REALIZING EDUCATIONAL RIGHTS

REALIZING EDUCATIONAL RIGHTS

Advancing School Reform through
Courts and Communities

ANNE NEWMAN

THE UNIVERSITY OF CHICAGO PRESS

CHICAGO AND LONDON

ANNE NEWMAN is a researcher at the University of California Center for Collaborative Research for an Equitable California. She is coauthor of *Between Movement and Establishment: Organizations Advocating for Youth.*

The University of Chicago Press, Chicago 60637
The University of Chicago Press, Ltd., London
© 2013 by The University of Chicago
All rights reserved. Published 2013.
Printed in the United States of America

22 21 20 19 18 17 16 15 14 13   1 2 3 4 5

ISBN-13: 978-0-226-07174-9 (cloth)
ISBN-13: 978-0-226-07188-6 (e-book)
DOI: 10.7208/chicago/9780226071886.001.0001

Library of Congress Cataloging-in-Publication Data
Newman, Anne, 1978– author.
    Realizing educational rights : advancing school reform through courts and communities / Anne Newman.
        pages ; cm
    Includes bibliographical references and index.
    ISBN 978-0-226-07174-9 (cloth : alkaline paper) — ISBN 978-0-226-07188-6 (e-book) 1. Right to education—United States. 2. Educational equalization—United States. 3. Educational change—United States. I. Title.
    LC213.2.N49 2013
    379.2'6—dc23
                                                                    2013013652

♾ This paper meets the requirements of ANSI/NISO z39.48–1992 (Permanence of Paper).

CONTENTS

ACKNOWLEDGMENTS

Writing is solitary work that can easily become isolating. When I think
about the years I have spent writing this book, I feel tremendously
lucky to remember first and foremost the people who showered me with
encouragement, insightful criticism, and well-timed diversions.

Eamonn Callan, Milbrey McLaughlin, and Rob Reich have contributed
enormously to the ideas in this book, and they have modeled for me how
to think rigorously and write analytically about educational philosophy and
policy. Bill Koski taught me the intricacies of school finance reform and
helped me understand when courts can make a difference. I am grateful for
the support of colleagues at Washington University's Department of Education, where I was a faculty member when I completed a first draft of this
book. I am also thankful for Ian MacMullen's astute feedback on an earlier
version of chapter 1. David Waddington has read every chapter of this book
multiple times and helped me make my arguments more compelling with
each reading. I will try to repay my enormous debt to him for years to come
as I read his works-in-progress.

The individuals I interviewed for the case studies taught me much about
rights claims in practice. Educational experts, legislators, and advocates
brought the significance of Kentucky's *Rose* decision to life by sharing their
experiences and files with me. The staff of Coleman Advocates for Children
and Youth in San Francisco have kindly invited me to meetings and shared
their experiences through numerous interviews so I might capture the evolution of their important work; I am particularly thankful for N'Tanya Lee's
insightful reflections about the role of rights discourse in their advocacy
efforts.

Elizabeth Branch Dyson at the University of Chicago Press has patiently
guided me through Chicago's publication process and provided invaluable

feedback so I might reach a broader audience. Michael Rebell is the reviewer every writer wants. I am indebted to him for his sage advice about strengthening my legal case study and for championing my work through the review process. I am also grateful for the feedback from an anonymous reader who pushed me to think more critically about the limits of court-based reform and rights discourse. Meg Murphy-Sweeney's astute editing made clunky text far more concise and clear in the final draft.

The National Academy of Education/Spencer Foundation Postdoctoral Fellowship allowed me to expand my data collection and provided a forum for getting very helpful feedback at earlier stages of this work. It also provided a one-year leave from teaching, and the months during that leave that I spent in Seattle were a rejuvenating change of scenery that enabled me to complete a draft of the book.

The arguments in chapter 1 build upon ideas I developed in "All Together Now? Some Egalitarian Concerns about Deliberation and Education Policy-Making," *Theory and Research in Education* 7, no. 1 (March 2009): 65–87; and in "A Democratic Framework for Educational Rights," *Educational Theory* 62, no. 1 (2012): 7–23. I am grateful to both journals for allowing me to reuse portions of these articles.

My parents and sister have enthusiastically cheered me on as this work became a book. I have a tireless marketing department in Nana, and I am grateful for her unbounded faith in me. And finally, to Stephen and Eleanor: Stephen has lived with this book-in-the-making for almost ten years and has read every draft. His feedback always surpasses his "one typo guarantee"; he has made each iteration of each chapter more crisp and clear. I am grateful for all of the hours he has spent talking about and reading my work. But I am even more grateful for his ability to keep me laughing and immensely happy. Eleanor was born just before I finished the penultimate draft of this book; she brings a previously unimaginable joy to my life.

R ights discourse has long been the language of reform in the United States. From the "unalienable rights" of 1776 to the rights revolution of the twentieth century (civil rights, disability rights, women's rights), significant social and political reforms have been sparked and sustained by citizens' appeals to rights. Education reform, especially in recent years, is no exception. As concerns about public education in the United States continue to mount, advocates of all stripes invoke rights to press for change. They speak of a right to school choice, of a right to math proficiency, of reading as the new civil right, and of the general right to learn. The moral heft of rights claims gives educators, parents, and politicians a powerful vocabulary (or as philosopher Ronald Dworkin put it, "political trumps") with which to express their frustrations with and hopes for public schools.[1] In the words of one advocate, "Part of what gets [parents] feeling strong is to say, 'You have a right!'"[2]

Rights claims persist in education reform discourse despite the significant challenges they face, practically and theoretically. As a simple legal matter, the U.S. Constitution is entirely silent on the matter of education, and the Supreme Court has denied claims to a right to education at the federal level.[3] State constitutions do guarantee students a public education, but usually without enough specificity to guide policy makers on what this right entails and how resources should be distributed to honor it. The uncertain place of educational rights in our legal system stems from the fact that the U.S. Constitution is understood to be a charter of negative rights—rights to be free from state interference and coercion in matters of speech, faith, and conscience. This interpretation of the Constitution guarantees no positive rights to particular social goods. This means that citizens have the right to decide what to believe and to express their chosen convictions. But

I

they do not have legally protected rights to housing, health care, or a decent education, at least not at the federal level as precedent now stands.

Beyond the practical obstacle of a legal tradition that has not supported positive rights, claims about educational rights also face thorny theoretical challenges. These difficulties arise because rights claims conflict with what is often understood to be the core of democracy: the principle of majority rule. Whereas this principle gives authority to the "will of the people," rights significantly constrain what a democratic majority may decide. Honoring the right to religious freedom, for example, prohibits a majority from making decisions that flout that individual right, however many people may wish to do so. Because rights have this countermajoritarian force, it is all the more important that they are "the Right rights," as Bruce Ackerman puts it.[4] This is especially true in the case of education policy making, given the long-standing tradition of local control of public schools in the United States.

So what case might be made for thinking about education as a "Right right" in a democracy? And how do rights claims shape education reform movements? My central purpose in this book is to advance the case for a right to education as a matter of political equality, and to consider how this right might be realized. My analysis is guided by two questions, one theoretical and one practical. My theoretical analysis addresses the question: *What is the place of a right to education in a participatory democracy?* The second part of my analysis then takes up the practical question: *How can this right actually be realized?*

In my theoretical analysis I develop a case for why an adequate K–12 public education warrants the status of a right in light of the ideal of equal citizenship, an ideal that stands at the core of American democracy. In this portion of the book (chapters 1–2), I argue for the necessity of this right as a precondition to deliberative democracy, and I outline what this entitlement should entail. I focus in particular on the deliberative conception of democracy, which centers on inclusive public discourse as the basis for collective decision making. This framework is fitting for my analysis for several reasons: because of deliberative theory's prominence within political philosophy; because it resonates with everyday notions of American democracy (like town hall meetings, for example); and because of scholars' frequent use of a deliberative framework when they are studying education policy making at the local level.

The early chapters of the book are largely addressed to political and educational theorists, and they consider enduring questions about what democratic ideals mean for the making of education policy. My central claim is that deliberative democracy cannot be sustained without a robust right to education—a right that I argue is not protected firmly enough in most accounts of civic education and deliberative democracy. Although educational rights have an uncertain place in American democracy, in chapter 3 I describe select moments in American history that illustrate that the idea of a right to education for equal citizenship has deep roots in our social and legal history.

The second part of the book addresses policy makers and advocates, in addition to theorists, and answers the pragmatic question of how we can realize a right to education. Through illustrative case studies, I consider two leading examples of democratic activism that advance a right to education. I first consider legal advocacy to examine what progress might result from taking educational rights claims to court. Legal advocacy is a major and growing avenue for education reform, as demonstrated by the school finance lawsuits that have now been filed in forty-five states. To examine the opportunities and challenges of court-based reform efforts, I focus on a landmark case from Kentucky, *Rose v. Council for Better Education*, which dramatically declared the entire state's public education system to be unconstitutional and affirmed students' right to an education that prepares them for citizenship, future educational opportunities, and the labor market. The decision is important because of the particular skills and capacities it enumerated as constitutive of an adequate education. It thus offers a useful point of comparison with my philosophical arguments by providing insights on the congruence and distance between moral and legal rights in the education arena.

I then examine a second leading type of activism to realize educational rights through the democratic process: the mobilizing efforts of community-based advocacy organizations. This form of democratic activism has quickly become a significant force in urban communities across the United States for reforming education policy, and for amplifying the voices of marginalized citizens in education politics. Local advocates often invoke rights claims for two purposes: as a means to empower parents to press for change, and as a way to compel politicians' attention. For an in-depth glimpse at rights claims in this context, I provide a case study of a highly successful advocacy organization in San Francisco that has been advocating for marginalized parents and youth for over thirty years. I consider how this organization employs rights discourse with parents and public officials, and to what effect.

Although legal advocacy and community organizing proceed in distinct venues with different norms, these case studies underscore how both types of activism are motivated by moral claims about educational rights. Understanding the moral warrant for such claims entails working across theory and practice. To this end, I do not offer the two case studies simply as instantiations of the theory I cover in the first portion of the book. Rather, I view the relationship between my theoretical arguments and the activism I examine as reciprocal. Democratic activism may showcase theory in action to some degree, but it also determines the practical value of theoretical arguments about educational justice. My analysis therefore considers how activism may bring theory to fruition, as well as how theory may need to be revised given the political, institutional, and legal constraints that shape advocates' work.

I am motivated to develop a case for a right to education by several gaps in the relevant literature across disciplines. In recent years political philosophers and theorists have increasingly argued for a constellation of positive welfare rights to ensure citizens' political equality, including rights to basic income, health care, housing, and employment.[5] These arguments differ in their details but share a foundational premise: if we are serious about achieving political equality in a democracy, then we must recognize and meet democracy's material preconditions. Giving citizens the right to vote is not enough, these arguments suggest, because hunger, homelessness, and poverty compromise, if not entirely undermine, the value of individuals' political liberties. Yet this literature's narrow focus on material goods, without any sustained consideration of education, rests on the dubious assumption that if citizens are decently housed, fed, and employed, they can participate in democracy on equal footing. This assumption fails to recognize the significant epistemic demands of democratic citizenship, and the importance of widespread, high-quality education to improve the conditions of democracy.

Significant contributions to educational philosophy have focused more squarely on the demands of civic education.[6] This literature is especially attentive to how civic education in a multicultural society may create tensions among parents, children, and the state, and how their competing interests might be balanced in the context of particular curricular and policy conflicts (related to sex education, homeschooling, or teaching evolution, for example). Yet its focus on balancing stakeholders' liberty rights in education policy offers little guidance about what the state must positively do to provide students with an adequate public education. This tends to leave important aspects of educational entitlements unsettled, including how strong those rights may be against majoritarian opposition. In addition, this literature typically locates arguments for civic education in the general context of a democracy, without specifying a particular conception of democracy (such as aggregative, deliberative, or representative). This generalist approach underdetermines the content of civic education. My focus on deliberative democracy addresses this problem and supports deliberative norms as ideals for collective decision making. But my rights-based approach calls into question whether deliberative education policy making can be done fairly today given the systemic background inequalities in educational opportunity and attainment.

From a policy perspective, the time is especially ripe for consideration of how a right to education might be realized. As school finance litigation continues to sweep across the states, litigators and scholars debate whether advocates should press for students' right to an equal education or to an adequate one. This discussion has focused scholarly attention on what type of education the state owes its citizens. But this work tends to be one-sided in its approach, given disciplinary divides: legal scholars wrestle with constitutional clauses to see what rights might be eked out from them, while political philosophers articulate what is morally best, whatever positive law might support. My analysis of the *Rose* case brings these two types of analysis together in recognition of the reality that ideals need legal and policy traction to be of use to education reformers. It also highlights the fact that court-based education reform is motivated by moral mobilization to a greater degree than is often recognized. My interdisciplinary approach enables a more comprehensive look at where ideals and practical constraints intersect in rights-based education reform efforts.

Finally, the case study of a community-based advocacy organization provides an important contrasting perspective to court-based efforts. Education researchers are increasingly recognizing the extent to which such organizations empower marginalized citizens to press for education reform.[7] This scholarship contributes to our understanding of how education reform can be community-driven; it also demonstrates how the reform process itself can further the ideal of a widely inclusive, participatory democracy. Yet existing literature does not focus much on the role of rights discourse in this process. By highlighting this dimension of advocates' efforts, my analysis sheds light on a key way community organizations can engage and empower parents to participate in education politics and policy making.

Taken together, my philosophical arguments and policy-oriented case studies demonstrate the need for a right to education and illuminate some promising paths to realizing this right. This analysis is especially timely given the growing chorus of concerns about educational inequities in the United States and lively debates about how they might be mitigated. The urgency of realizing a right to education is also underscored by the leading conferences, philanthropic initiatives, and advocacy efforts dedicated to rights-based education reform in recent years.[8] Its importance is arguably best demonstrated, though, by the many citizens who leverage rights discourse to bring about educational change because "When you say 'It's a right,' it is undeniable. It is what should happen."[9]

My overarching aim in this book is to bring various disciplinary and methodological approaches to bear on a topic that is critically important now, philosophically and practically speaking. Americans consider public education to be the most important equal-opportunity welfare good. Whatever its legal viability, rights discourse persists as a valuable vocabulary with which to express our aspirations for a better public education system and, by extension, a better democracy. By exploring the role of rights claims in both theory and in practice, I aim to advance understanding of the complicated relationships among moral claims, educational justice, and public policy.

PART I

Educational Rights in Theory

CHAPTER ONE

Education Policy Making in the Shadow of an Enduring Democratic Dilemma

How can a democratic government both honor popular will and promote just public policies, given that collective decisions may compromise some individuals' rights? Political philosophers have focused a great deal of attention on this classic tension between democratic decision making and rights.[1] Far less attention has been directed at the implications of this tension in the education arena, where it deeply shapes individuals' life chances. The significance of the tension in this arena is evident when we ask moral questions about how we should make education policy in the United States. For example, should local majorities rule when it comes to setting property tax rates and passing school bonds, given that these decisions significantly affect school quality? Or should they rule when it comes to developing school-assignment policies that dictate which children learn together, and therefore the level of diversity in schools?

Resolution of such issues may involve difficult trade-offs between democracy, understood as rule by the people, and rights, understood as constraints on popular rule in the name of justice. But these competing principles are rarely given equal consideration in education policy making. Through elected school boards and local school councils, democratic majorities have wide latitude over important education policies. Although the federal government in the United States regulates many aspects of public education (for example, civil rights protections and accountability policies for student achievement), the long-standing norm of local control safeguards citizens' authority over significant determinants of educational opportunity. Citizens' authority is evident in recent state ballot initiatives curtailing affirmative action and bilingual education, and in the more regular decisions voters make about tax policies that affect school funding. To see the extent to which the principles of justice may be disregarded in these collective decisions, we need look no further than the well-documented disparities in educational opportunity that track race, class, and geographic borders.

Leading accounts of democracy, even those with egalitarian intentions, often fail to protect the interests of marginalized students. This failure not only exacerbates educational injustices, but it also undermines the legitimacy of democratic decision making itself. The respective priority accorded to democracy and justice in the education policy process are thus out of balance. My central purpose in this chapter is to call attention to this imbalance and to propose a way to correct it: we should regard education, which prepares individuals for equal citizenship, as a fundamental right that is shielded from democratic politics far more than existing practices permit, and far more than most theories recognize as necessary.[2]

I locate my arguments about a right to education in the context of deliberative democracy for two reasons. First, deliberative democracy, which stipulates that public policy should be decided through inclusive public discussions, has become the most widely debated view of democracy among political theorists. And its academic prevalence is spreading across disciplines as empirical scholars test its principles in different real-world contexts, including education politics. Deliberative enthusiasts look to school board meetings and local school councils to observe deliberation in action, and they advocate more and better deliberation to improve the education policy process.[3] As interest in deliberation grows among education scholars and reformers, it is especially important to consider how well this approach to policy making serves less advantaged students—a concern that researchers overlook when they assume that deliberations are egalitarian.

Second, deliberative theory is an apt framework for thinking about a right to education because it reflects an idealized site of democratic citizenship: the New England town meeting, where citizens discuss public policy with an eye to the common good. According to this ideal, government is not the business of experts but the work of engaged citizens. If this popular vision of democracy is to be realized, citizens must be provided an education that enables them to participate in collective decision making as civic equals. Whether citizens have access to such demanding education should not be left to the sway of majoritarian politics to the extent that it often is, in both theory and practice.

I largely endorse deliberative theory; my purpose in advancing a rights-based approach to educational opportunity is not to challenge deliberative theory as a democratic ideal. Rather, by highlighting the scope and significance of the educational prerequisites of deliberative democracy, I aim to show why deliberative policy making is ill-suited to remedy educational inequalities and inadequacies when those prerequisites go unmet. This reality does not undercut the merits of deliberative ideals. But it does call into question the prevalent appeals to deliberative norms in contexts where these norms are unlikely to mitigate—and may very well exacerbate—the considerable educational injustices that obtain in the United States today.

THE GOALS AND CHALLENGES OF DELIBERATIVE THEORY

Deliberative theorists have varying conceptions of the proper aims, processes, and outcomes for collective decision making. Differences among theorists arise, for example, with respect to the importance of achieving consensus; the types of reasons citizens should offer to explain and defend their views to each other; and the relative priority assigned to procedural fairness (how collective decisions are made) and to outcomes fairness (what is decided).[4] I set aside these differences for now to focus on goals that are common across conceptions of deliberation; these goals shed light on the theory's educational implications.

Deliberative theory can be understood as an egalitarian response to majoritarian, vote-centric views of democracy, which I refer to as economic theories.[5] Economic theories of democracy are driven by observations and assumptions about the realities and limits of democracy in practice, in contrast to deliberative theory's focus on how democracy should function. According to the economic view of democracy, politics is a competition among self-interested individuals seeking to advance their discrepant interests. Joseph Schumpeter's view of democracy, though extreme, exemplifies this position. Schumpeter is deeply pessimistic about citizens' capacity for intelligent political participation (he calls most people's political opinions "an indeterminate bundle of vague impulses"), and he concludes that democracy is better off with limited citizen engagement.[6] In his view, democracy is little more than a matter of aggregating citizens' preferences and abiding by the majority's opinion.

Deliberative theorists rightly reject this strictly majoritarian approach to collective decision making as the "numerical version of might makes right," as Amy Gutmann puts it.[7] As she and other critics emphasize, majoritarian theories of democracy are morally problematic for two reasons. First, they are insensitive to the fact that some viewpoints are unlikely to constitute the majority opinion. This relegates certain groups to permanent minority status, so their interests lose out in democratic politics over and over again. Second, by assuming that citizens' preferences are largely fixed and that they maximize self-interest, majoritarian views of democracy discount the possibility that citizens might revise their opinions and become more public-spirited when presented with others' perspectives. Such assumptions are useful for the formal modeling of political behavior but are ethically troubling because when individuals form their starting preferences, their views may be benignly ill-informed or malevolently prejudiced.

To correct for these problems, deliberative theorists advocate widely inclusive public discourse as the best way to make collective decisions. As they see it, public forums provide an opportunity for all viewpoints to receive consideration, whatever the size of their support base. Many deliberative theorists also argue that if citizens are given a chance to share their beliefs and hear from others, they will come to have a more capacious understanding of the common good and will revise their views accordingly. In theory then, deliberation improves upon the mere procedural equality of voting by ensuring that marginalized groups have a fair hearing and by prompting citizens to become more informed, tolerant, and public-spirited.

Deliberative ideals hold great promise for education policy making, especially compared to the alternatives. Under a majoritarian vote-centric model, minority interests may have little chance of gaining serious consideration in the policy process. In addition, citizens' most significant opportunity for political expression might come at the polls, where secrecy provides cover for self-interest. The 1978 passage of Proposition 13 in California, which capped property tax rates, is especially illustrative of the problems endemic to a vote-centric model of democracy. Some supporters of this taxpayers' revolt might have been disinclined to publicly defend their position, which prioritized individual financial concerns over collective support for public schools. By contrast, when public deliberations are the locus of decision making, citizens are mutually accountable for the exercise of their shared authority.[8] In the case of Proposition 13, childless homeowners would have to encounter and grapple with the perspectives of families with children attending public schools. This public and more transparent process better honors the notion of public schools as a collective good, which is an ideal increasingly challenged by market-based reforms, privatization, and the educational arms race of college admissions in privileged communities.[9] Deliberating about education policy, it seems, might help revitalize the notion of public education as a public good.

Yet deliberative theory faces significant criticism because of deliberation's potential to exacerbate existing social and political inequalities. This line of criticism is important to consider from the vantage point of educationally disadvantaged individuals, especially when it comes to collective decision making about education policy.

Egalitarian critics worry that citizens have unequal chances to influence public deliberations because the norms for participating privilege certain communication styles. As a talk-centric form of collective decision making, public deliberations aim to hold citizens mutually accountable for the expression of their beliefs through the norms of public reason. These norms place limits on how individuals engage with each other in the public sphere; various conceptions of deliberation advance different norms, but some limits are common across theories. For example, citizens are expected to refrain from making sectarian claims that are rooted in particular belief systems (such as religious frameworks); they should make appeals that are rooted in reason rather than emotion; and their preferences should be guided by concern for the common good rather than self-interest.[10] The purpose of such limits is to facilitate discussions among citizens who may have widely diverse political, religious, and moral commitments, and to ensure that citizens can participate in deliberations on equal footing.

Egalitarian critics take issue with the norms of public reason, and some worry more broadly that a discursive policy process is inherently elitist. They argue that deliberation privileges the communicative styles of more advantaged citizens (for example, white, middle-class men), at the expense of people whose manner of speaking does not follow Enlightenment views of rationality, whose worldview is rooted in a religious framework, or who have less social and political power.[11] In short, critics charge that because it privileges nonsectarian logic and reasoning over emotional pleas, religious claims, and personal narratives, deliberative theory is culturally biased.[12]

Concerns about cultural bias have understandably dominated most criticism of deliberative theory. To be sure, the challenge of ensuring that all citizens are equally recognized in public discussions may be an intractable problem for deliberative theory.[13] Beyond inequalities that stem from communicative norms, we must also be attentive to how inequalities in resources impact citizens' standing in public discussions—particularly educational inequalities in the context of decision making about education policy. Many deliberative theorists acknowledge that certain background conditions must be met if deliberations are to proceed fairly, but they typically do not give educational opportunity sustained attention.[14] The question of why educational inequalities are particularly problematic in deliberative settings is also underexplored, especially when it comes to deliberations about education policy itself. Leading theories of deliberative democracy fail to shield educational rights from democratic diminishment, and this failure has significant consequences for deliberative determination of education policy.

PROTECTING EDUCATIONAL RIGHTS
FROM DELIBERATIVE DEMOCRACY

While most deliberative theory (like political theory more broadly) pays scant attention to its educational implications, Amy Gutmann and Dennis Thompson's work is a notable exception. Gutmann is especially attuned to the civic importance of education in a participatory democracy given her earlier seminal work on the subject. Gutmann and Thompson state that deliberative democracy "goes even further than most other forms of democracy" in its educational demands.[15] Yet even their approach to collective decision making does not sufficiently safeguard educational entitlements from majoritarian politics. This calls into question the fairness of applying deliberative norms to education policy making and portends more significant problems for deliberative theories that are less attentive to education.

Gutmann and Thompson advocate a hybrid conception of deliberation to balance concern for a fair democratic process with attention to the justice of deliberative outcomes.[16] Their theory does not privilege principles of procedural fairness or substantive fairness. Instead, "both interact dynamically in ways that overcome the dichotomy between procedure and outcome."[17] This hybrid approach, coupled with Gutmann's concern for education, makes their conception of deliberation a fitting test case for the question, Can deliberative theory both safeguard individuals' right to education and respect democratic authority? After all, a purely procedural view of democracy would be a straw-man counterpoint to my arguments for a firmer right to education, while a purely substantive view would not grapple enough with concerns about democratic participation.

To achieve this balance between rights and democracy, Gutmann and Thompson endorse welfare minimums for basic social goods like education, health care, and income. These minimum thresholds establish a floor for citizens' entitlements to public provisions and then leave room for democratic decision making above that floor. Gutmann and Thompson emphasize that an egalitarian standard that guarantees equal outcomes for all citizens is too demanding, both democratically and practically. So too is John Rawls's difference principle, according to which basic social goods would be distributed to maximize the well-being of the least well-off. For example, if we were to fund health care until the health of the least well-off citizens is maximized, we would have few resources left for other goods. Even a more modest outcome-oriented proposal to provide health care so that all individuals reach a baseline of good health may be unrealistic, Gutmann and Thompson argue.[18]

To be sure, there are sound practical reasons to resist robust welfare rights in conditions of scarcity. Thick rights in such contexts could effectively deny democratic bodies the latitude to decide and to reconsider how resources should be allocated. Gutmann and Thompson's approach at first pass is compelling because it ensures that citizens have an adequate level of basic resources without implausibly guaranteeing equal outcomes in these domains.[19] This approach mirrors how Gutmann balances education entitlements with democratic authority in her earlier work, where she advances a "democratic authorization principle" that enables democratic bodies to determine the level of public provisions for education while forbidding them via a "democratic threshold principle" from denying any citizen the education necessary to participate effectively in the democratic process.[20] Upon closer inspection, though, this approach is deeply problematic because it relies on the deliberative process to determine what counts as an adequate education: "The best way of determining what adequacy practically entails may be a democratic decision-making process that follows upon public debate and deliberation."[21] Because of the tight correlation between education and political influence in deliberative settings, by giving deliberative bodies the discretion to decide the scope of what counts as an adequate education, this view provides little protection for the interests of educationally disadvantaged citizens.[22]

A deliberative process for determining basic rights might work well in other policy arenas, like health care. Gutmann and Thompson demonstrate this possibility by describing the case of an Arizona woman who argued before the state legislature that it should fund a liver transplant she critically needed.[23] The fact that she did not have private health insurance did not, in and of itself, compromise her political influence. She could still stand before her elected officials and discuss health care funding as their civic equal. When individuals in need of the social good at stake are not necessarily politically disadvantaged by that need, deliberatively determining social minimums could yield a fair process and outcome. Housing is also relatively distinct from political equality; with the exception of conditions of homelessness, one's relative home value usually has little direct bearing on one's ability to influence public deliberations.

On the other hand, deprivation of access to an adequate education more often than not converges with the condition of being uneducated in ways that curtail political agency. Deferring to deliberative bodies to decide what constitutes an adequate education, then, renders those citizens most in need of the social good at stake disadvantaged in the very process that should improve their lot. Deliberative ideals for education policy making may be

compelling in contexts where educational opportunities are already great
enough for all citizens to participate in collective decision making as civic
equals. But given the systemic educational inequalities and inadequacies
in the United States, attempts to implement these ideals are more likely to
exacerbate rather than mitigate the injustice they aim to redress.

If deliberative theory is to have traction in nonideal contexts, independently specified educational rights are required that are just as robust as the
theory's expectations for citizens' political participation. Deliberative ideals
imply a robust right to education, but as Gutmann and Thompson's theory
illustrates, this right is too often underspecified or insufficiently shielded
from the deliberative process itself—even among the theorists who are
most concerned about educational opportunity. Gutmann and Thompson
are certainly not blind to the importance of education to the viability of
their theory, but like many advocates of deliberation, their theory rests on
an overly optimistic appraisal of how nonideal conditions bear on deliberations about education policy.

Two facets of educational distribution today are especially sobering re-
minders of how significantly background inequalities shape public deliberations about education policy and why a more robust rights-based approach
is warranted. First is the well-documented reality that public schools are
increasingly segregated by race and class. As Gary Orfield and colleagues
report, in the 2009–10 school year, 74 percent of African-American public
school students attended schools that were majority minority; meanwhile,
white students attended schools that were on average 75 percent white.[24]
This racial segregation is highly correlated with class-based segregation. For
that same school year, African-American students attended schools where
almost 64 percent of students were poor, while white students attended
schools where 37 percent of students were poor on average.[25] These statis-
tics underscore the reality that when citizens discuss education policy in
their school community, they are likely to be talking with people who look
very much like themselves. Deliberative theory's vision of policy discussions among diverse citizens is a far-fetched aspiration given these patterns
of segregation and the structures of local control that reinforce them.

Second is the reality that the outcomes of public deliberations about
education policy carry very different consequences for citizens depending
upon their access to exit options, such as transferring their children to a
private school or relocating to a place with better public schools. A central
tenet of deliberative theory is that citizens are mutually accountable for
the positions they advance in public discourse and that they view them-

selves as bound to deliberative outcomes.[26] Yet the exit options provided by private schools and suburbanization in the United States significantly erode the mutual accountability that theorists idealize; the only citizens who are fully bound to education policy decisions are those with limited financial means.[27]

Deliberating about education in such imperfect conditions runs the risk of exacerbating educational inequalities—and then the political inequalities that follow. Without independent specification of what a proper education entails, we may end up with (and we arguably have) a deliberative arena in which educational adequacy is defined at a point so low that it effectively disenfranchises some citizens. James Bohman captures this problem when he notes that disadvantaged citizens are in a "double bind" when it comes to challenging prevailing public measures of what counts as an adequate floor for public functioning and resources: to challenge such standards requires "precisely what political poverty makes difficult: the capacity to challenge dominant standards in public debate and discussions."[28] This is arguably most true of education, given the nature of the relationship between educational opportunity and political equality.

THE RELATIONSHIP BETWEEN EDUCATION AND POLITICAL EQUALITY

Making informed decisions about representation and public policy requires a host of abilities, including analytic reasoning skills and the ability to distinguish sophistry from sound argument. This is even more true in a deliberative democracy that expects citizens to contribute to agenda setting, in contrast to a vote-centric democracy that simply asks citizens to cast ballots for representatives.

The crux of the relationship between education and political equality centers on the types of advantages that education affords citizens in public discourse. People who have comfortable housing, lucrative employment, and good health care may participate in deliberation more easily than those who are less well-off in these respects. Moreover, severe deprivation in any of these welfare domains may impede political participation altogether. Yet inequalities with respect to housing, income, or health care do not result in deliberative inequality per se. Having a bigger house, a more lucrative job, or better health care does not directly confer superior deliberative skills upon citizens.

By contrast, education is directly tied to deliberative influence, and it is not possible to neutralize educational inadequacies to restore political equality without addressing educational deficits head on. The political disadvantage that follows from having poor reasoning skills or limited literacy, for example, is hard to remedy without addressing these problems directly. Moreover, educational inequalities cannot be readily contained for the sake of achieving political equality in public forums. How could well-educated citizens refrain from using their skills in deliberations? Basic income, on the other hand, is largely instrumental to deliberative influence, and the well-being it provides can be achieved through various means, such as public assistance for food and housing. By contrast, the quality of citizens' education directly affects their effectiveness in public deliberation, and nothing short of giving citizens the requisite skills can compensate for their lack thereof.

A few caveats are necessary here. Some citizens may secure the skills that constitute an adequate education outside formal schooling because these skills are not the sole province of formal education. And not all schools successfully teach students the requisite deliberative skills. Even many well-funded schools may fail on this front. Moreover, a charismatic personality may more than compensate for educational disadvantage in some deliberative settings. Yet the possibility of autodidacts and compelling personalities cannot vindicate miserly provisions for public education. Nor do the deficiencies of civic curricula today diminish the importance of the state's responsibility to do better on this front. After all, for the vast majority of citizens, educational opportunity is limited to the offerings of the public system. When public schools fail them, a significant portion of the population is likely to be severely disadvantaged in the political sphere.

The tight link between education and political equality is poignantly expressed in Supreme Court Justice Thurgood Marshall's dissenting opinion in *San Antonio Independent School District v. Rodriguez*, in which the majority opinion refused to recognize a federal right to education.[29] In addition to finding no legal ground for such a right, the majority expressed concern that recognizing a right to education would open the floodgates to myriad other welfare rights. Marshall refuted the Court's slippery-slope argument by contending that education is distinctively tied to individuals' ability to exercise constitutional liberties, including free speech and the right to vote, and to participate in politics more generally: "Education may instill the interest and provide the tools necessary for political discourse and debate. Indeed, it has frequently been suggested that education is the dominant factor affecting political consciousness and participation."[30] His dissent highlights how the meaningful exercise of political liberties is inextricably tied to educational opportunity—a connection that is even tighter in a deliberative democracy, where one's reasoning skills and ability to communicate determine one's opportunity to have political influence.

What does this mean for the prospect of fair deliberations to determine minimum educational entitlements? Citizens who lack a decent education are more likely to be marginalized in deliberative forums across the board, whatever the subject of discourse. Yet their disadvantage is compounded in deliberations about education policy itself—a problem that theorists have largely overlooked by focusing on other policy domains to demonstrate deliberative theory's feasibility. This disadvantage is not merely a technical one in the sense that citizens may lack the skills to participate effectively. More deeply, citizens who have only experienced woefully inadequate schools may understandably have an impoverished view of the ambit of educational possibilities. For example, a history teacher who had taught in south Los Angeles for seventeen years came to believe that asking the state via litigation to provide each student with a textbook was too demanding.[31] Social scientists have reported similar reactions from students in failing schools; their isolation from privileged communities circumscribes their vision of school reform, so they make only depressingly basic requests. As Ian Shapiro emphasizes, individuals have to be able to envision better circumstances for themselves, and when the distance between here and there is so vast, "certain goals will be abandoned from your field of aspirations."[32]

This problem could certainly impede community-based reform efforts in other policy domains where social goods are provided in deeply segregated contexts. Citizens who have never experienced adequate health care or decent living conditions may come to see their lot as the norm rather than cause for moral outrage. Yet these lowered expectations are especially pernicious when it comes to education, given education's strong correlation with access to a constellation of social goods and opportunities that compound educational advantage: admission to selective universities, remunerative and rewarding employment, health care, leisure time, and so on.[33]

Given these high stakes, relying on a deliberative process to determine the minimum threshold for educational entitlements seems patently undemocratic in light of background inequalities today. But staking out a more determinate threshold without resort to a deliberative process does pose justification problems. As Gutmann and Thompson underscore, any such approach "must show that outcome-oriented principles in some meaningful sense take priority over a deliberative democratic process. This seems a more than Herculean task."[34] Yet if we are willing to be more agnostic about how best to institute the educational preconditions that make collective decision making truly democratic, then the task of justification becomes far less difficult. As Harry Brighouse has put it, if our goal is to make education policy in a way that treats children as moral equals, "Democracy may be this method, but it may not."[35]

WHAT HAPPENS IN EDUCATION DELIBERATIONS? A LOOK AT EMPIRICAL FINDINGS

Empirical studies of what happens when citizens deliberate about education policy confirm the theoretical concerns I have highlighted. Public deliberation may violate egalitarian ideals at two distinct points: procedurally, with respect to the formal inclusion of citizens in public forums; and substantively, with respect to deliberative outcomes. Studies of deliberation about education policy indicate failures on both counts. These failures are unsurprising given the nonideal contexts in which deliberations about education policy occur. Nonetheless, it is worth calling attention to this empirical evidence given many deliberative theorists' overly sanguine view of the background conditions that shape deliberative policy making and of how those conditions bear on the possibility for a fair process and outcomes. Studies that focus on education deliberations are few in number, but several leading projects illustrate the problems that arise.

Consider Archon Fung's much-cited study of local school councils (LSCs) in Chicago.[36] In 1988, the Chicago Public School system decentralized school governance to LSCs created at each school site. The LSCs are composed of elected citizens, teachers, and principals. This path-breaking reform gave LSCs decision-making authority over school reform plans, budgets, and the hiring and firing of principals, thereby shifting significant power from the district's central office to local communities. Fung examines LSCs as deliberative bodies and is largely optimistic about the degree to which they realize deliberative theory's core ideals. His celebratory assessment of LSCs is warranted to some degree. They do empower citizens to make decisions about important features of their school community, and they add more and different voices to local policy-making efforts. Empirical data, however, suggest a much less rosy story if we take seriously the goal of inclusion.

Although Fung reports that participation rates in LSCs (measured by the number of parental candidates vying for LSC seats) were roughly the same across poor and advantaged neighborhoods, representation within LSCs was heavily tilted toward the well-off.[37] This bias is especially dramatic with respect to educational attainment. Only 13 percent of LSC members in a probability sample lacked a high school diploma, while 34 percent of adults in Chicago had no high school diploma.[38] Fung reports that this city-level educational bias is repeated within LSCs at particular schools: at schools whose students almost all come from low-income families, LSC members have educational levels similar to those of the overall Chicago population.[39] It could be argued that having better educated LSC members is beneficial to low-performing schools, assuming they advocate for the interests of all students at a school. Yet from a democratic perspective, it is worrisome that educational inequalities translate into uneven representation at the local level, where parents should be able to participate in education policy making most easily.

The research that Fung draws from indicates that LSC participation was uneven in another way that warrants attention. The racial and ethnic composition of each school council reflected the composition of its student body in most schools—a positive finding, to be sure.[40] Yet there is a notable exception to this outcome that is troubling given deliberative theory's egalitarian ideals. In integrated schools, white parents and community members were significantly overrepresented on LSCs: they constituted 85 percent of LSC members in schools where only about 50 percent of the student population was white, on average. This overrepresentation was repeated at the city level: whites constituted 40 percent of LSC members across Chicago, while only 11 percent of the student population was white.[41] These data indicate an outcome that runs counter to the very core of deliberative ideals: that equal representation according to race was achieved in segregated contexts, but not in more diverse school communities.

Given the extent to which public schools are segregated today, proportional participation by race in segregated areas could be seen as a step in the right direction. Yet the situation is still deeply problematic. De facto segregation challenges the appropriateness of deliberative policy making, and the possibility that deliberation might work well in homogenous settings largely misses the mark of its proponents' intentions. Deliberation should bring diverse citizens to the same table if public forums are to be meaningfully inclusive and directed at a capacious understanding of the common good. Public forums composed disproportionately of educated citizens within communities that are already significantly segregated by race are a distant second best.

Research that examines how citizens address each other within deliberative forums, and the outcomes of their discussions, also yields troubling results. In their study of local school boards in South Carolina, Lorraine McDonnell and M. Stephen Weatherford arrived at findings that mirror data from Chicago on LSC participation bias. In one county they studied, well-educated, middle-class citizens outnumbered other participants once public forums moved from the neighborhood to the larger community level.[42] Their data further suggest that middle-class interests dominated the substance of discussions. For example, they note that there was no sustained conversation about racial disparities in educational opportunity despite the obvious salience of this issue to local education politics.[43] They conclude, more cautiously than Fung, that deliberative forums are potentially inclusive venues for honoring collective commitments to public education, but they acknowledge the ongoing challenge of incorporating marginalized citizens and interests. Shapiro conveys the significance of this challenge when noting how residents of Connecticut defeated a statewide plan to reduce segregation in public schools via deliberations that marginalized inner-city residents.[44]

These empirical studies, though a limited sample, reveal the problems that surface when deliberative theory is applied to education policy making in the context of significant background inequalities. Of course educational inequalities are not the sole cause of political marginalization in these instances; the unequal distribution of other social goods and opportunities may compound educational disadvantage, yielding an entanglement of welfare disadvantages that impede some citizens' political participation and influence. Biased deliberative norms may also disenfranchise citizens, whatever their educational attainment. Redistributing educational opportunity then is unlikely to single-handedly even out participation disparities and political influence in public forums. Yet given the significant and enduring correlation between educational attainment and civic participation, educational entitlements warrant far more attention than existing accounts of deliberation grant them.[45] Without firmer educational rights, deliberative ideals have traction only when educational injustices are slim or nonexistent (for collectively deciding finer curricular matters when basic educational rights are already realized, for example). This is a significant limitation for a democratic theory that aims to help ameliorate background inequalities. To overcome this limitation, deliberative theory should incorporate a right to education that is determined prior to and independent of the deliberative process.

I have argued that deliberative bodies are not reliable guardians of students' right to an education that prepares them for equal citizenship. This naturally raises a practical question: What alternative institutions and policy processes might do a better job? I take up this question in the second half of the book, where I consider two different types of democratic activism that advance educational rights. But before I turn to the practical matter of how to realize a right to education, it is necessary to consider what this right should entail and to elaborate on its warrant. These are the issues to which I turn in the next chapter.

CHAPTER TWO

The Shape of a Right to Education

If we should treat education as a preconditional right to enable fair deliberative decision making, what should this right include? To answer this question, it is necessary to grapple with the classic tension between rights and democracy that I highlighted in the previous chapter.[1] Rights claims convey unparalleled moral and political urgency because of their privileged place above majority will. Yet their function as "political trumps," as Ronald Dworkin has put it, presents a significant justification problem for those who advocate welfare rights, including educational rights.

Rights claims have become ubiquitous in education reform discourse. Yet little work to date has focused a philósophical lens on the substantive argument for a right to education, its democratic implications, and what this entitlement should include.[2] The gap is especially notable in two bodies of literature that I draw on: political philosophy and the philosophy of education.

Although political philosophers have argued for a constellation of socio-economic rights (such as housing, basic income, and health care) to ensure citizens' political equality, they have largely ignored education. Their focus on material goods fails to recognize the significant epistemic demands of deliberative citizenship, and the importance of an adequate education to improve the conditions of democracy. But the democratic rationale with which theorists defend rights to other social goods applies equally well, if not more strongly, to education.

Philosophers of education frequently appeal to rights in their accounts of what civic education encompasses and how educational authority should be shared among stakeholders. But their analysis often understates what educational rights entail and the nature of the state's obligations to realize them. This is because theorists have focused primarily on determining the proper scope of state and parental authority over children's education.[3] This perspective tends to relegate the state's role to that of a mere backstop whose chief responsibility is to compensate for parental dereliction (for example, by regulating homeschooling). Such analysis provides far too thin an account of the state's obligations to students and far too anemic a conception of educational entitlements. Moreover, most accounts of civic education are situated in the general context of a liberal democracy and do not specify a more particular conception of democracy—whether aggregative, deliberative, or representative. This generalist approach also underdetermines the demands of citizenship to which educational rights should be tailored.

In this chapter I provide a thicker account of the right to education and the state's positive obligation to realize this right in view of what citizenship entails in a deliberative democracy.[4] My analysis proceeds in three parts. I begin with a brief overview of rights theory to call attention to how education is sidelined in existing accounts of welfare rights, and to discuss why it merits a place alongside the other social goods covered by this literature. Next I defend the deliberative view of citizenship as the proper framework in which to situate educational rights. Finally I turn to the educational demands of deliberative citizenship.

In describing a right to education for equal deliberative citizenship, it is not my purpose to develop a complete civic curriculum. Rather, I describe the general contours of this right by focusing on the skills associated with meaningfully exercising free speech and voting rights, which illustrate the conditions that facilitate equal citizenship. To this end, I draw on theoretical accounts of what civic education should entail as well as empirical studies of the particular civic skills that education can foster.

My arguments in this chapter will not resolve the enduring tension between rights and democracy. This tension remains the backdrop to my analysis rather than its direct subject. Yet when theorists do address this tension directly, any plausible resolution must take seriously arguments of the sort that I advance about a right to education. Democratic institutions clearly cannot thrive unless citizens receive an education tailored to the demands of citizenship. These demands involve unavoidably high standards whose realization should not be left to the sway of majoritarian politics, and thus justify the use of rights claims in the education arena.

THREE GENERATIONS OF RIGHTS

Scholarship on rights broadly addresses what interests count as rights, who may be entitled to them and why, and the duties these entitlements imply.

Because I am interested in the democratic rationale for a right to education, I focus on the subset of rights theory that is concerned with the legitimacy of rights claims in a majoritarian democracy.[5] As I have emphasized, rights limit the scope of democratic authority in order to protect individuals' fundamental interests. Where does education fit among these interests, and what challenges do claims to educational rights face?

Rights theorists often refer to three "generations" of rights, which helpfully sorts rights according to the entitlements they guarantee and the duties they impose on others.[6] First-generation rights, or liberty rights, delineate what the state cannot do to citizens. These rights prevent government intrusions into citizens' private lives but are silent about what social goods, if any, the state positively owes to citizens. Educational theorists often focus on first-generation rights to determine the boundaries of state control of public schools given parents' liberty to guide the upbringing of their children. This line of inquiry addresses pressing policy problems such as how to manage conflicts between parents' religious beliefs and school curricula.

Liberty rights address only one part of the state's obligation to students. Concern for liberty rights, for example, may be one factor in determining whether schools should defer to parental preferences about teaching evolution so as not to violate parents' right to exercise their religious beliefs. Yet this does not tell us about the state's obligation to cultivate citizens' science proficiency. A more robust type of right is needed to capture students' educational entitlements that extend beyond noninterference by the state.

The right to education with which I am concerned falls into the category of second-generation rights, which also include entitlements to other welfare goods like housing, health care, and employment. These rights claims are controversial for several reasons. Because welfare rights are often rooted in theories of justice, they can be used to criticize socioeconomic conditions and to advocate redistributive policies—a contested arena that first-generation rights are unlikely to enter.[7] Although some scholars have argued that the distinction between first- and second-generation rights is overblown since both require state funding and enforcement, welfare rights are more controversial because they are perceived to require greater state intervention and resources.[8]

Welfare rights can be defended on instrumental grounds (they are necessary for the meaningful exercise of liberty rights), or on the basis of intrinsic necessity (they are constitutive of human dignity).[9] Both justifications face significant criticism. One criticism comes from Robert Nozick's libertarian view, which regards efforts to realize welfare rights as encroachments on more fundamental liberty rights. According to this view, the only real rights individuals can be said to have are liberty rights.[10] Others have argued that human rights to goods like decent pay and health care should not be called rights because they are impossible to realize in many contexts. As philosopher Maurice Cranston put it, "Such things are admirable as ideals, but an ideal belongs to a wholly different logical category from a right."[11]

The American constitutional landscape presents additional obstacles to welfare rights claims. Because the U.S. Constitution enumerates negative rather than positive liberties, American rights theorists do not have firm textual support in the Constitution with which to validate their claims.[12] Although there is a rich tradition of legal scholarship arguing for socioeconomic rights via the 14th Amendment's equal protection clause, judicial support for such rights has been very limited.[13] Welfare rights claims also raise concerns about creating a bottomless pit for state spending and denying democratic bodies the authority to decide and reconsider how to spend limited public resources. Beyond questions of constitutionality and cost, some critics argue that the pervasiveness of "rights talk" degrades political discourse and undermines personal responsibility. From this perspective, Mary Ann Glendon writes that advocates' reliance on rights talk often amounts to "careless habits of speaking" that obstruct careful thinking about what should count as rights and who should have the duty to fulfill them.[14]

Finally, in contrast to first- and second-generation rights, which are held by individuals, third-generation rights are group rights. Some goods and opportunities fall into this category because they are collectively created and enjoyed, like clean air.[15] Other group rights are afforded to minority populations to protect their culture and practices (for example, the right to be taught in one's native language).[16]

Because the right to education that I advocate applies across subgroups to all citizens in the United States, my analysis proceeds within the framework of a second-generation welfare right. The central and ongoing challenge for theorists who advocate welfare rights is to define more narrowly and defend more thoroughly what counts as a right, given the litany of opposition to second-generation rights.

EDUCATION IN WELFARE RIGHTS LITERATURE

As rights claims proliferate in the political arena, political philosophers and theorists have renewed debates about the warrant for and scope of welfare rights. Yet the bulk of welfare rights theory is curiously inattentive to education compared to its concern for a host of other social goods.

Within academic philosophy, Philippe Van Parijs's proposal for unconditional and universal basic income has sparked much debate about the material basis of a just society, while other philosophers argue for rights to health care, housing, and employment.[17] But this literature gives little or no attention to education. Jeremy Waldron, who has written extensively about welfare rights, mentions education only briefly and does not distin-guish its importance from that of health care, employment, and social se-curity.[18] Lesley Jacobs similarly defends welfare rights and justifies their redistributive implications, but his consideration of education does not ex-tend beyond characterizing it as a collective need (along with health care) for which the state should provide.[19]

Other accounts of welfare rights focus on basic entitlements to physical security and subsistence and relegate education to a distant and secondary focus.[20] Legal scholars have focused more attention than many philosophers on the right to education, especially in response to the Supreme Court's 1973 decision in *San Antonio Independent School District v. Rodriguez* (discussed in detail in chapter 3), but their arguments understandably tend to concentrate on the narrower issue of how positive law might support a right to education rather than on the right's moral warrant.

The relative silence about education in the philosophical treatment of welfare rights is especially surprising given theorists' egalitarian and demo-cratic motivations. For example, Carole Pateman grounds her defense of a right to basic income in citizenship concerns: "a basic income would help remove impediments to freedom, help citizens enjoy and exercise citizen-ship, and help provide the security required if citizenship is to be of equal worth to everyone."[21] Other philosophers similarly defend rights to hous-ing, health care, and employment in recognition of the fact that some threshold of material well-being is necessary to exercise political liberties and ensure political equality. T. H. Marshall's analysis of the civic, political, and economic rights that flow from the ideal of equal citizenship is a classic argument in this camp. It dedicates more, though still limited, attention to education.[22] In a similar vein, Corey Brettschneider has recently argued that certain welfare rights (like the right to a job and to basic income) are central to democratic self-government. But he too gives education only passing at-tention.[23]

Although equal citizenship is my primary concern, welfare rights litera-ture's lack of sustained attention to education is also notable considering the well-known economic returns to education. Research overwhelmingly shows that citizens who receive more and better education enjoy a host of benefits such as better health care, greater job satisfaction, and higher rates of personal savings.[24] Correlation and causation may be difficult to untangle in this context because well-housed, fully employed, and healthy citizens likely have greater access to good schools. But the relevant point is that a high-quality education helps facilitate the material well-being that welfare rights theorists emphasize, making the absence of sustained attention to education in this literature all the more notable an omission.

Explanations for this relative silence about education are unconvincing, but they do point up why education merits distinct treatment in the rights literature. One justification stems from concerns about the democratic rationale for welfare rights. If welfare rights are rooted in their ability to facilitate democratic participation, what if it turns out that a particular social good does not have this effect after all? Given this possibility, some theorists reject an instrumental defense of welfare rights that hinges on those rights' procedural value to democracy.[25] But the instrumental argument for a right to education is very strong, contra the Supreme Court's reasoning in the *Rodriguez* decision. Given the vast body of research that demonstrates the tight correlation between individuals' educational attainment and political engagement, there is little reason to believe that education is unrelated or only weakly related to the meaningful exercise of political liberties.[26]

A second reason that might justify the absence of education in welfare rights theory is that it could be argued that rights to other goods, like basic income, sufficiently ensure access to an adequate education. Yet this argument is not compelling for reasons highlighted by the capabilities approach to distributive justice. As Amartya Sen emphasized in his seminal paper "Equality of What?" individuals have different abilities to translate material goods into well-being.[27] This is most simply demonstrated by the fact that two people are unlikely to be equally sated or healthy when given the same quantity of food or health care. Capability theorists therefore insist on cultivating the skills and capacities that constitute individuals' well-being instead of focusing only on the distribution of material resources.

This view of justice shows why a right to basic income is not a reliable stand-in for a right to education. Setting aside personal spending preferences, some people may not be able to translate a given sum of money into adequate educational opportunities because the force of other needs is greater, or because quality schooling options are inaccessible to them. Similarly, realizing one's right to shelter cannot be counted on to ensure one's access to high-quality schools. Public provisions for housing, for example, would likely do little to ensure children's educational opportunity if neighborhood school assignment policies are in place and if school quality is tightly correlated with housing prices. To be sure, access to other welfare goods has a significant impact on students' achievement, and educational opportunity often is undermined by the symptoms of poverty.[28] Making students' right to education meaningful requires attention to their broader living conditions. Yet what this well-documented reality demonstrates is that a right to education alone is not sufficient; it does not mean we do not need education entitlements alongside other welfare rights.

Educational theorists have given more attention than political theorists and philosophers to the notion of education as a right, but their treatment of the concept often does not grapple enough with the tension between educational rights and democratic authority. Nor does it focus on the scope of the state's duties to realize those rights. Theorists have advanced different conceptions of educational justice, such as whether students are entitled to an equal education or to an adequate one; whether merit should have a role in the distribution of educational opportunity; and whether private schools and other types of parental partiality are justified.[29] Yet when theorists make claims about the scope of students' entitlements, they tend not to say much about the strength of those claims against majoritarian opposition. Silence on this front then leaves the force of their rights claims in democratic contexts uncertain. This is evident in the ongoing debate about whether students are entitled to an adequate or to an equal education, which largely proceeds without much concern for how either the equity or the adequacy perspective might be defended against majoritarian opposition.[30]

Because advocates on both sides of this equity-versus-adequacy debate regard their view as a requirement of educational justice, they presumably would not yield to majority opposition. But they often fail to provide a defense of the priority of their view over democratic preferences to the contrary. And as I argue in chapter 1, theorists like Amy Gutmann who do address the rights-democracy tension in greater detail are often overly sanguine about the inclination of democratic majorities to do justice by all students. This optimism leads them to dismiss too quickly the tension between rights and democratic rule, leaving rights claims on uncertain ground.

In sum, welfare rights claims are especially vulnerable to the criticism that they are imprecise, rhetorically inflated, and poorly defended. Advocates of educational rights must take seriously such criticism, particularly the concern that rights undermine democratic governance. In view of these concerns, in the following sections I describe the foundational skills and capacities that a right to education should foster. Since my focus is on equal citizenship, I begin by elaborating the view of citizenship to which I tailor this right.

THE DEMANDS OF DELIBERATIVE CITIZENSHIP

Deliberative democracy offers an aspirational but not utopian framework in which to situate a right to education in that it expects neither too much nor too little of citizens. On the one hand it does not assume that active political participation is a duty that everyone must fulfill at the expense of their private commitments. On the other hand it affirms that individuals can play a significant role in democratic governance if they wish, and it does not underestimate the educational demands of equal citizenship. Deliberative democracy is thus situated between two more extreme interpretations of citizenship, neither of which provides a fitting framework for a right to education in a liberal democracy.

On the too-demanding end of the spectrum is the civic republican view of citizenship, which treats political participation as a duty that all individuals must fulfill. Aristotle's view, though extreme in its assumption that human flourishing depends on active citizenship, illustrates this perspective: "We must not regard a citizen as belonging just to himself: we must rather regard every citizen as belonging to the state."[31] Political liberals rightly reject the revival of this view by some contemporary civic republicans because it leaves little space for individuals' private commitments and pursuits. If the democratic state is to accommodate and respect individuals' diverse life plans, then it must accept that some individuals will choose to retreat from public life.

The problems that follow from such a demanding view of citizenship are especially evident in its educational prescriptions. The views of the American revolutionary Benjamin Rush clearly illustrate the potential dangers here: "Our country includes family, friends, and property, and should be preferred to them all. Let our pupil be taught that he does not belong to himself, but that he is public property."[32] Few contemporary thinkers advocate such an extreme position. Yet even a more moderate civic education that teaches that all students must actively participate in politics undercuts the respect for diversity that a liberal democracy should uphold. Moreover, as Harry Brighouse emphasizes, such a curriculum is not necessary to realize political equality. He uses the analogy of an egalitarian distributing material resources to argue that although individuals should have an equal share of the goods at hand, equality does not require that they actually use the resources to which they are entitled. By the same token, all students should be educated so that they are prepared for democratic participation, but civic equality does not require teaching that they must engage in politics.

If teaching all individuals that it is their duty to participate in politics asks too much, several prominent political theorists—most notably John Rawls and William Galston—defend a view of citizenship that is far too thin. Though Rawls says very little about civic education in *Political Liberalism*, his terse description of it presents an anemic view of what it entails. In recognition of the diversity of citizens' values, he advances a view of politics that does not rest on any single comprehensive doctrine or worldview. It "leaves untouched all kinds of doctrines—religious, metaphysical, and moral—with their long traditions of development and interpretation," to advance a view of the political community that is neutral among "reasonable" belief systems.[33] This view of politics rejects public policies that are justified by a particular religious framework, and it endorses only rationales rooted in "public reason," understood as reasoning that is accessible to all. For example, it would reject abortion policy rooted in Catholic doctrine but accept policy cast in terms of legal precedent. It is beyond the scope of my analysis to discuss what Rawls considers reasonable and whether it is possible to maintain neutrality among diverse ways of life.[34] But Rawls's approach notably does lead to an impoverished view of civic education in contrast to what deliberative theory can support.

Rawls's concern for citizens' diverse private commitments leads him to reject a civic education that promotes personal autonomy, most basically understood as individuals' ability to reflect critically and independently on their commitments and beliefs. Rawls endorses a circumscribed form of autonomy, political autonomy, which pertains only to how individuals reason about decisions in the public sphere. He rejects an education aimed at a more encompassing conception of autonomy because it could encroach on some citizens' religious and cultural commitments that do not value critical reflection.[35] As a result, the civic education he endorses is limited to the bare basics, including knowledge of constitutional and civic rights so that, for example, people "know that liberty of conscience exists in their society and that apostasy is not a legal crime."[36] As Eamonn Callan underscores, this amounts to little more than encouraging citizens to know their rights, a goal that is "modest to the point of banality."[37] Of course students should know that apostasy is not a crime, but this is hardly adequate preparation for democratic citizenship.

It is doubtful that Rawls's view of politics could be sustained by such a thin civic education; as a number of theorists have argued, his theory depends on a far more significant and less culturally neutral education than he acknowledges.[38] But whether or not Rawls's views on education are sufficient for his political theory, the civic education he explicitly endorses is far too anemic for any viable conception of democratic citizenship.

Galston's concern for accommodating diversity also leads to a conception of civic education that is far too thin. Galston rejects education for autonomy, personal or political, out of deference to parents who wish to impart beliefs to their children without encouraging critical reflection. He writes: "As a political matter, liberal freedom entails the right to live unexamined as well as examined lives—a right the effective exercise of which may require parental bulwarks against the corrosive influence of modernist skepticism."[39] Yet this position backs Galston into the same corner in which Rawls ends up: his view of civic education, intended to be maximally accommodating, is far too thin. Callan describes the problem well:

> The necessary point of departure in identifying the ends of civic education is an account of the responsibilities of the citizen and what she must learn to discharge them well. Is there a defensible account that would make the relevant responsibilities and their educational prerequisites undemanding? Galston provides none, and I do not believe there could be one, at least for the general circumstances of citizens in modern liberal democracies.[40]

The skills and capacities that enable equal citizenship in a democratic state, and even more so in a deliberative one, are not minimal. If the republican conception of citizenship and civic education is too thick, Rawls's and Galston's views are too thin.

Deliberative democracy offers a view that mediates between these extremes. It certainly is not undemanding, given its goal of fostering a widely inclusive, discursive form of politics that tracks the common good. But it does not insist that individuals sacrifice their private commitments to privilege political participation. In short, it enables citizens to have a significant role in self-government if they so choose and recognizes the educational demands of this role without devaluing or overriding private interests and pursuits. And it requires the cultivation of autonomy as a matter of equal citizenship, as I next argue.

TWO TOUCHSTONES OF EDUCATION
FOR EQUAL CITIZENSHIP

Given the demands of deliberative citizenship, what skills should a right to education encompass if it is to foster political equality? It is beyond the scope of this section to lay out a complete curriculum for equal citizenship. My more modest aim is to provide a sketch of the fundamental skills and capacities that all citizens should possess to be civic equals. This focus bounds my analysis in two ways. First, my unit of analysis is the individual and not the democratic state, because the state's perspective is the wrong view for considering how to advance equal citizenship. The democratic state does not need to have each of its citizens prepared to exercise their political liberties, but more minimally needs only enough engaged citizens to sustain the democratic process. State interests, then, cannot underwrite an education to which all citizens are entitled. I accordingly set aside questions about how civic education may bolster state stability in order to focus on the education to which all citizens are entitled as a matter of political equality.

Second, my focus on political equality also limits my discussion to the skills that have direct bearing on citizens' standing in public deliberations about public policy. There are myriad virtues and skills that, if possessed by some number of citizens, might make for a more just state. For example, we would likely be better off if more citizens had an enduring interest in learning about different religions and cultures. Yet this virtue is not essential for every citizen to possess as a matter of political equality. Lack of curiosity about other ways of life does not necessarily diminish one's political standing or that of others, so long as individuals are reasonably tolerant. My focus on individual competencies essential to political equality thus excludes many worthy skills and virtues that could improve the health of the democratic state and individuals' lives, but that are not strictly necessary for the realization of political equality.

Within these parameters, I outline the contours of a right to education given the skills needed to exercise two foundational democratic liberties: the right to vote and the right to express oneself freely. I focus on these two liberties because of their centrality to democratic citizenship and because of the educational implications that follow directly from them. As Richard Arneson and Ian Shapiro emphasize, "Guidelines for educational policy are implicit in the rationale for freedom of expression."[41] Educational prescriptions also follow closely from the right to vote. Although conceptions of deliberative democracy privilege public discourse as a method for deciding public policy, voting may play a role when consensus cannot be reached. In such cases, deliberation is still a critically important precursor to voting because it can significantly affect individuals' understanding of the common good and thus influence the decisions they make at the polls.[42]

Taken together, the skills needed to exercise meaningfully the right to free speech and the right to vote provide a sense of the foundational and enduring features of what a right to education must encompass in a deliberative democracy (and would certainly improve the conditions of democracy today, too), even as particular aspects of a right to education must shift as social expectations and the demands of citizenship evolve over time. To inform my analysis, I draw on educational theory, social science research, and school finance lawsuits in which civic skills were central to determinations about what counts as a constitutionally adequate education.

COGNITIVE AUTONOMY FOR MEANINGFUL VOTING

Citizens who can recognize and wrestle with complex policy issues must possess the ability to think critically, reflectively, and independently—skills that constitute cognitive autonomy. The place of autonomy in civic education has been debated at length because of its tension with liberalism's core commitments to toleration and diversity.[43] This debate typically focuses on how civic education to cultivate autonomy affects individuals' private commitments, and whether this influence can be justified in a liberal state in which autonomy is not a universal value. Numerous theorists have taken a stand on this issue, either to justify or to deny the impact of an autonomy-fostering education on individuals' religious and cultural commitments.[44] I set aside this well-covered aspect of the debate in order to focus on the less discussed issue of how autonomy enables political equality in the public sphere.

There is a significant degree of overlap between autonomy's influence in the public and private spheres. As Gutmann writes, the cultivation of autonomy for use in the public sphere "cannot be neatly differentiated from the skills involved in evaluating one's own way of life."[45] Autonomy facilitates equal citizenship in ways that parallel its value in the private sphere, and recognition of this overlap leads many theorists to focus on defending education for autonomy from parents who object that it interferes too much with their private commitments. My rights-based approach concentrates instead on the state's obligation to provide a civic education that cultivates autonomy as a matter of civic equality, which I argue is an indefeasible commitment. This view of the state's obligation is a stronger position than many educational theorists explicitly take in their accounts of civic education.[46]

A rights framing also calls attention to how democratic majorities should be constrained to protect individuals' entitlement to an education that cultivates autonomy. This point is often lost in theorists' focus on parental objections that arise from particular religious or cultural commitments. Whereas parents are often presented as the chief obstacle to the development of children's autonomy, the public sphere presents a wider array of threats to autonomy, such as politicians' rhetorical devices and advertising by profit-seeking corporations. Cognitive autonomy is a necessary buffer against manipulation by these parties, as the case of voting illustrates. Citizens who are cognitively autonomous have the analytical skills to evaluate the veracity of political rhetoric, to consider whether claims advanced in the public sphere support the common good or sectarian interests, and to determine whether candidates' campaign promises are consistent with their view of social justice. The ability to evaluate others' claims carefully is foundational to substantive political agency, understood as the capacity to exercise one's political liberties in a meaningful, not merely procedural, way. Cognitive autonomy enables individuals to carry out these evaluations—to develop a view of what course public policies should take, and to assess proposed options accordingly.

Developing and acting on this sense of purpose in the public realm parallels what Rawls termed "deliberative rationality," which is part of individuals' capacity to develop a sense of what is the best life for them. Though Rawls describes deliberative rationality in terms of individuals' ability to make sound decisions about their private good, his description applies well to individuals' choices about public policy issues as well. The rational plan for an individual, argues Rawls, is the plan one decides on after carefully reviewing all relevant facts and forecasting which option is most likely to meet one's goals.[47]

Applied to the public realm in a deliberative democracy, the rational plan would be to endorse the candidate or policy that best represents the common good after conducting a discerning review of available information and considering future consequences of present choices. As Rawls acknowledges, there are significant information problems here because individuals can be mistaken about what their own good is.[48] This is no less true in politics, where voters may come to see that their intuitions about a candidate's character or a policy's impact were dead wrong. Yet these problems are largely unavoidable and do not diminish individuals' agency in a way that jeopardizes their political equality. As Rawls puts it, in the end an individual's choice "may be an unhappy one, but if so it is because his beliefs are understandably mistaken or his knowledge insufficient, and not because he drew hasty and fallacious inferences or was confused as to what he really wanted."[49] Parallel goals for political decision making can be drawn from this: when voters regret their decisions, that regret should stem from unavoidable information problems rather than from the inability to reason carefully about their choices.

The ability to think critically and the habit of making well-informed political decisions give rise to another virtue that is part of cognitive autonomy: intellectual flexibility. This is of central importance in a deliberative democracy. Whereas economic theories of democracy assume that citizens' preferences are rigidly fixed, deliberative theory presupposes that citizens' opinions are revisable in light of compelling new evidence and arguments. If voting in the context of a deliberative democracy is to be more than a tallying of fixed beliefs, citizens' openness to new information and arguments is key. This openness is central to Amy Gutmann and Dennis Thompson's account of mutual respect in a deliberative democracy: "It is the character of individuals who are morally committed, self-reflective about their commitments . . . and open to the possibility of changing their minds."[50]

Although existing empirical studies of the relationship between education and civic participation usually do not discuss autonomy directly, they document skills that are constitutive of autonomy and necessary for capable voting.[51] Studies confirm not only that "education by far is the strongest correlate" of civic engagement, but also that it fosters skills that strengthen the quality of individuals' engagement.[52] For example, one study found that college entrance increases voter participation by 17 to 22 percent, and that additional years of secondary schooling significantly increase individuals' support for protecting the free speech of certain minority groups.[53] These findings suggest that education can promote cognitive autonomy for voting by broadening the range of ideas that voters are willing to hear, thereby making for a more independent, informed, and tolerant electorate. Another study documents more specifically how education affects individuals' reasoning skills, finding that individuals with a stronger baseline of civic knowledge are better able to understand political events and incorporate new information into their perspective—capacities that are required for the autonomous exercise of the right to vote. Informed individuals are also more likely to vote on the basis of substantive issues and candidates' political performance instead of perceptions of personal character.[54]

Of course literacy, numeracy, and a basic understanding of history, economics, science, and literature are foundational to understanding political and social issues in an ever-evolving world, and to deliberating these issues with diverse fellow citizens. The importance of these skills cannot be overestimated, as Meira Levinson reminds us, because if citizens "cannot do these things, then they will not be able to construct, analyze, or take thoughtful positions on the multitude of issues facing adults in the political world."[55]

One study found that the strongest predictor of multiple measures of political engagement is verbal aptitude; it had significant influence on voting rates, participation in community service, and attempts to persuade others of one's political commitments.[56] Such skills are necessary to ensure political equality, but they are not sufficient. The demands of deliberative citizenship go beyond mastery of basic skills to prescribe a civic disposition characterized by openness to new evidence and ideas in the face of moral disagreement. One can meet and far surpass the basic threshold for rudimentary skills and knowledge and be closed to facts and arguments contrary to one's beliefs. Such obstinacy disrupts political equality to the extent that some citizens will find that their arguments fall on deaf ears. Those who hold rigidly fixed beliefs may also find themselves at a political disadvantage if they cannot consider the merit of evidence and logic that challenge their views. Political equality demands an intellectual give-and-take among citizens. Literacy, numeracy, and analytical skills are foundational to making sound electoral choices, but they must be supplemented by intellectual flexibility.

Plaintiffs in recent school finance cases have contended that adequate education for civic equality entails more than mastery of basic academic skills, and they have called on the courts to consider a broader array of student outcomes connected to the meaningful exercise of citizenship rights and to duties like voting and serving on a jury. Some courts have responded favorably, recognizing the especially onerous cognitive demands of citizenship today. For example, the trial court in a recent New York school finance case found that: "An engaged, capable voter needs the intellectual tools to evaluate complex issues, such as campaign finance reform, tax policy and global warming. . . . Similarly, . . . jurors may be called on to decide complex matters that require the verbal, reasoning, math, science, and socialization skills that should be imparted in public schools."[57] And as I discuss in chapter four, the Supreme Court of Kentucky similarly recognized that the demands of citizenship extend beyond basic math and literacy skills in *Rose v. Council for Better Education*, a decision recognizing students' right to an education, which includes "sufficient knowledge of economic, social, and political systems to enable the student to make informed choices."[58]

The necessity of an education for cognitive autonomy is also demonstrated by the vices of inequality that it thwarts. Consider the position of citizens who lack the ability to evaluate political rhetoric carefully and independently. They are vulnerable to manipulation by a number of sources that may violate their political equality and that of others, whether by way of religious intolerance, racial prejudice, or sexism. Clearly these vices—

especially when people cling to them with unreflective fervor—jeopardize the political standing of citizens who become the target of prejudice. Of course perfectly autonomous citizens may adopt ugly beliefs, too. Yet the spread of such beliefs to the point where they saturate politics is much less likely if citizens are less vulnerable to indoctrination. Citizens who lack cognitive autonomy are also at a disadvantage to the extent that their interests are limited by inherited beliefs that run counter to current facts, future possibilities, or the common good. Although they may not lack formal political equality if they are members of a majority group, such individuals lack substantive political agency.

Cognitive autonomy is not an unqualified good in spite of the virtues and skills it promotes and the vices it thwarts. As Callan emphasizes, there is an important balance to strike when promoting the development of citizens' critical reasoning skills: we do not want hypercritical nihilists any more than we want unthinking patriots.[59] Galston's concept of civic education errs too far on the side of uncritical patriotism by promoting a moralizing, whitewashed history that affirms the status quo in the name of political stability.[60] Civic education of this sort runs counter to the core of deliberative democracy by frustrating, if not impeding, serious reflection about political issues. Yet danger from the opposite side is equally threatening, as pervasive cynicism may lead individuals to a "political dead end."[61] The challenge is to guide the development of critical reasoning so individuals see its political function, to enable citizens to be "both civically engaged and uplifting while remaining genuinely critical."[62]

PUBLIC REASON FOR FREE SPEECH

One of the chief purposes of public reason is to regulate public discourse. Like autonomy, public reason encompasses multiple skills and virtues, and it has received a great deal of attention in liberal theory, especially deliberative theory, given its talk-centric approach to collective decision making. Because deliberative theory is predicated on the beliefs that everyday citizens can be involved in policy decisions via public discourse and that this discourse will advance a common good, it depends on discussions that are characterized by mutual respect and public reason. As Rawls explains, "Public reason is characteristic of a democratic people: it is the reason of its citizens, of those sharing the status of equal citizenship."[63] The types of arguments that fall within the scope of public reason is a contested issue. Setting aside debates about the permissibility of religious arguments in public deliberation, public reason asks citizens to express their views in terms that are widely accessible, reason-based, and focused on the common good.

Public reason's norms for civic engagement serve political equality. As Gutmann and Thompson emphasize, because deliberative decisions bind all citizens, it is only fair that the discourse that yields these decisions proceeds in terms that are mutually justifiable and acceptable. Public reason thus promotes the virtues of reciprocity and wide public accountability.[64] To participate in public discussions, then, citizens need to understand the boundaries of acceptable language and forms of engagement. This involves comprehending the difference between self-interest and the common good, and refraining from using the latter as a mask for the former. It also necessitates learning how to make rational, evidence-based claims in lieu of resorting to emotional manipulation. As Gutmann and Thompson underscore, these intellectual and moral demands are hardly facile ones; developing students' "civic integrity and civic magnanimity" extends far beyond the teaching of basic academic skills.[65]

An important caveat is needed here. Although in ordinary times citizens should follow the norms of public reason in public deliberations, there are times when public reason may have to be abandoned in the name of political equality. Citizens must learn this through civic education: that forms of discourse that depart from the norms of public reason may be justified when deliberative forums unjustly and systematically prevent certain perspectives from receiving a fair hearing. It is for this reason that Rawls condones the abolition and civil rights movements' use of religious arguments that otherwise violate his view of public reason. He writes: "citizens are to be moved to honor the ideal [of public reason] itself, in the present when circumstances permit, but often we may be forced to take a longer view."[66]

Gutmann and Thompson also acknowledge that such departures in the form of passionate, immoderate speech may be necessary if disadvantaged citizens are to overcome background inequalities that impede their full inclusion in political decision making.[67] Yet overuse of immoderate speech would collapse deliberative democracy into interest group pluralism, wherein citizens act strategically without moral constraints. Departing from the norms of public reason is justified only when that departure is a necessary means to realize ends consistent with deliberative ideals.

The importance of knowing how to use public reason, and when alternatives are necessary, is exemplified by what it takes to exercise freedom of speech effectively. If the exercise of this right is to have a meaningful impact upon public discourse, then citizens must understand what language will be received by their peers as accessible and compelling, and what language will be dismissed as unintelligible or outlandish. Ideally speaking, pontificating about political conspiracies, cults, or pseudo-scientific claims is unlikely to win the day in public discussions that follow deliberative norms. So as a matter of political equality, citizens must know the difference between such claims and ones that will be accorded consideration.

Most important, adhering to the norms of public reason keeps public discourse centered on mutual respect and inclusiveness, the core values of a deliberative democracy. At the same time, citizens must understand that they should not naively abide by these norms when doing so would leave them politically marginalized by grave injustices. Such marginalization would amount to a denial of their freedom of speech and implicitly condone or even perpetuate inequalities. In order to create conditions conducive to equal and inclusive deliberation, citizens have to learn when alternative means are necessary to achieve that end.[68]

As is the case with autonomy, empirical studies of the correlation between education and civic participation do not measure directly individuals' understanding of and willingness to use public reason in policy deliberations. But existing studies do document closely related skills that are central to the meaningful exercise of free speech. As noted above, for example, the number of years of education individuals receive is positively correlated with their support for protecting the free speech of certain minority groups.[69] This support is foundational to the mutual respect and inclusiveness that are the core of public reason, and that enable all citizens to exercise meaningfully their free speech rights.

Concern for the public good as opposed to private interest is also central to public reason, and studies show that education can be influential in this respect too. For example, one study found that more knowledgeable citizens are more likely to consider the state of the national economy as opposed to their personal economic situation when voting.[70] Another study found that certain college majors influence students' inclination to value political influence, understood in a public-spirited sense, over personal financial success.[71] Finally, there is a strong correlation between education and what researchers have called "enlightened political engagement," which includes political tolerance—a value that is central to public deliberations that follow the norms of public reason.[72]

In sum, understanding the rationale for public reason and learning to exercise it in the public sphere must be central features of a right to education for equal citizenship. Citizens must also learn when alternative forms of language and advocacy are necessary to promote greater political equality—for example, when systemic inequalities prevent public reason from fostering a widely inclusive view of the common good.

Development of students' cognitive autonomy and their command of public reason not only has theoretical warrant in view of the demands of deliberative citizenship; social science research demonstrates that these capacities are correlated with educational attainment and are significant predictors of the degree and quality of citizens' political participation. Without these skills citizens cannot meaningfully exercise political liberties like voting and free speech. Although I have tailored my arguments about these skills to a conception of a democracy that is more deliberative than current practices in the United States, the civic skills I have outlined are central to bringing about a more just political process in the current context, too.

Because of theorists' concern for figuring out the proper scope of parental authority over children's education, few accounts of civic education focus in a sustained way on the state's positive obligations to realize students' right to education. Attention to this issue is especially important today, when the most pressing educational problems stem not from unchecked parental authority, but rather from gross state negligence.

As the landmark case that I discuss in chapter four, *Rose v. Council for Better Education*, illustrates, when public education is badly in need of reform, the state's most urgent duty may not be to rein in parents but to remedy systemic institutional failures. Of course, parents do have a critically important role to play; the state cannot single-handedly realize students' right to education. The task requires the efforts of multiple stakeholders. As Waldron underscores, realization of moral rights is not accomplished in simple two-party relationships but involves "successive waves of duty."[73]

A right to education for equal citizenship is not a utopian proposition. I next turn to both historical and legal scholarship that ascribes to the state the duty to realize students' right to education. Although assigning such an obligation to the state, especially to the federal government, is often challenged as inconsistent with American social and legal norms, at various moments in time, the United States has come close to recognizing the existence of a right to education for reasons that parallel the arguments I have offered about equal citizenship.

CHAPTER THREE

Historical Attempts to Advance
a Right to Education

rguments for a right to education for equal citizenship can seem very idealistic. Rights claims are highly vulnerable to this criticism because it is unlikely that many of the entitlements that reformers advocate will be realized. As Maurice Cranston asks, in reference to the United Nations Universal Declaration of Human Rights, "How can the governments . . . where industrialization has just begun, be reasonably called upon to provide social security and holidays with pay?"[1]

It is true that by rooting my arguments in deliberative democratic theory, I have tied my analysis to a view of politics that is more aspirational than it is reflective of current conditions. This leaves my arguments vulnerable to the criticism that they are merely utopian. One possible response to this criticism is that feasibility constraints should not dictate what counts as a moral entitlement.[2] My purpose in this chapter, however, is to demonstrate that educational rights claims grounded in concerns about deliberative citizenship have had significant traction outside the realm of theory.

To this end, I look to history to respond to the criticism that robust educational rights claims in the United States are just an intellectual fantasy. These claims have deep roots in social and legal history and have animated significant reform efforts. Although education is not mentioned at all in the U.S. Constitution, its importance to the ideal of equal citizenship is widely recognized. Americans look to public schools to compensate for a range of inequalities, making schools the "answer to the European welfare state, to massive waves of immigration, and to demands for the abolition of subordination based on race, class, or gender."[3] The importance that Americans ascribe to public education, some argue, makes it a de facto national right.[4] And although the civic purposes of public schools are often eclipsed by concern for economic returns, reformers have long expected schools to prepare students for the rights and responsibilities of deliberative citizenship. These expectations have fueled historically important efforts to expand, improve, and equalize educational opportunity—efforts that at times have come close to securing a federal right to education.

My historical review of such efforts is necessarily selective. I focus on reforms targeted at the federal level because this is where education entitlements attached to citizenship have been most vigorously debated—at least until the Supreme Court's 1973 ruling in *San Antonio Independent School District v. Rodriguez*, which denied a federal right to education.[5] Before turning to that decision, I discuss education proposals from three historical periods during which foundational questions about rights, citizenship, and democratic entitlements were reconsidered: the Revolutionary period, Reconstruction, and the New Deal.[6] Although reformers during these periods did not always express their goals explicitly in terms of rights, their efforts were clearly motivated by a sense that students are entitled to a sound education by the state.

By highlighting historical reform efforts, I aim to dispel the notion that educational rights claims do not comport with our legal and social history.[7] Charges of utopianism notwithstanding, such claims are an enduring part of our politics, and as historian Carl Kaestle reminds us, examining even "noble failures" to advance a right to education can be useful for charting the course ahead.[8]

EDUCATION AND THE AMERICAN REVOLUTION: MAKING CITIZENS "REPUBLICAN MACHINES"

Americans' enduring concern for public education can be traced back to the earliest of conversations about American citizenship and its educational implications. Although the American revolutionaries did not give education the constitutional status of a right, they clearly recognized the civic role of schools as they grappled with fundamental political questions: What sort of relationship would citizens have with their government? How would they achieve political stability? To answer these questions, early American leaders drew heavily on classical views of republicanism, particularly the notion that there is a common good and that citizens have a duty to participate in politics to realize it. As historian Gordon Wood emphasizes, such views "added a moral dimension, a utopian depth, to the political separation from England."[9]

This view assigned to schools the task of creating virtuous citizens who would put country before self. Indeed, to the revolutionary thinkers, realizing republican ideals was largely an educational project. A 1775 statement by church minister Moses Mather illustrates well the civic importance ascribed to schools: "The strength and spring of every free government is the virtue of the people; virtue grows on knowledge, and knowledge on education."[10]

Although they lacked consensus on what republican virtue entailed and how best to cultivate it, the American founders shared a belief that citizens' virtue was central to the success of the new republic, but also extremely fragile. They espoused great faith in the political utility of spreading knowledge, while they harbored deep anxieties about citizens' character. This confluence of hope and apprehension is clearly reflected in educational proposals from the period, which were largely directed at keeping vice at bay.

Given concerns about citizens' moral character, much of the discourse about education during the revolutionary period was motivated by political expedience. Benjamin Rush's views exemplify this orientation; as he saw it, schools should "render the mass of the people more homogeneous and thereby fit them more easily for uniform and peaceable government."[11] The educational writings of Noah Webster and Thomas Jefferson similarly focus on inoculating citizens from the vices that might undermine republican virtue. For Webster, this included promoting uniform spelling and pronunciation to cultivate national pride and identity. Jefferson focused on the education of an elite cadre of citizens whom, he assumed, voters would have the good sense to elect.[12] To be sure, such proposals demonstrated far more concern with political stability than with equality. And because access to formal schooling before the common school movement was limited or nonexistent for women, African-Americans, and poor students, the educational ideals espoused during this period were intended only for a small fraction of the population.

Nonetheless, calls for a "more general diffusion of knowledge," which Jefferson's 1779 proposal for a more expansive schooling system in Virginia exemplified, had an egalitarian bent for their time in that they sought to educate a broader swath of citizens in support of self-government. And some education reformers advocated the spread of knowledge to promote liberty more so than uniformity, as a 1797 essay on education emphasizes: "An enlightened nation is always most tenacious of its rights."[13] Using schools to "render the mass of the people more homogenous" was surely one route to political stability, but so too was training citizens to understand, exercise, and protect their liberty. If the new republic was to eschew aristocratic government in favor of widely shared political authority, then citizens had to know how to exercise that authority and guard it from encroachment. In

James Madison's words, "A popular government without popular information or the means of acquiring it is but a prologue to a farce or tragedy."[14]
This focus on an informed, engaged, and public-minded citizenry carries
through to the ideals advocated by present-day deliberative theorists, some
of whom trace their views back to the Constitution itself.[15]

Early thinkers' seemingly unbounded faith in schools' ability to cultivate virtue for republican citizenship faded in the years following the revolution, which perhaps contributed to education's absence from the federal
Constitution.[16] One possible explanation for this waning optimism is that
commercial interests gave rise to factions that splintered civic unity.[17] This
might have prompted political leaders to shift their attention from schools
to technocratic ways to control factions, including Madison's proposal
in *The Federalist Papers* for a system of checks and balances among the
branches of government.[18] Another possibility is that Americans were on
their best civic behavior at the height of the revolutionary crisis and then
were less dutiful when external threats seemed less imminent.[19] The causes
of this shift are complex, but its implications for education are clear: the
framers focused far more on the institutional design of representative government than on public schooling despite their elevated rhetoric about how
education is integral to the success of democracy.

This shift is seen in the outcomes of early attempts to secure public
support for education. For example, Thomas Jefferson's visionary "Bill for
the More General Diffusion of Knowledge" would have established a three-
tiered education system in Virginia, from primary schooling through college, in order "to illuminate, as far as practicable, the minds of the people
at large."[20] Yet Jefferson's plans were never realized. Local wrangling over
the control and financing of public schools defeated his bill; ironically it
was the victim of the very problems it aimed to fix.[21] Jefferson's one educational plan that was adopted—establishment of the University of Virginia—made way for the education of an elite group of future leaders rather
than the general public. Likewise, at the federal level, reformers' efforts to
institutionalize their grand ideals met little success. Plans for a national
university were never realized in spite of repeated and passionate pleas by
George Washington and by every president following him until John Quincy
Adams.[22]

Measured against the lofty rhetoric about education's purpose, relatively
little was accomplished in the republic's early years to realize these ideals,
as Kaestle underscores: "While the great ideas of the American Revolution
had some impact on the popular mind and found much practical expres-

sion . . . many local institutions were largely unchanged. This was the case with schooling."[23] But the elevated rhetoric about the civic importance of public education forged a tight link between schooling and the practice of democratic citizenship in American political discourse, which kept in circulation the idea that state provisions for education were essential to democratic self-rule. Policy proposals from the post–Civil War period more directly advocated federal responsibility for education as a constitutional duty tied to equal citizenship.

POST–CIVIL WAR ATTEMPTS AT
FEDERAL EDUCATION POLICY

Legal scholars and historians often focus on policy proposals from the Reconstruction era when tracing the lineage of the federal government's role in public education.[24] Of course the preceding common school movement significantly expanded educational opportunity too and gave Americans' educational ideals an institutional expression that augmented the jumble of charity, religious, and private schools that had been in place.[25] Yet the common school movement unfolded state by state without substantially increasing the federal government's commitment to education. By contrast, Reconstruction reformers specifically aimed to hold the federal government responsible for more robust education provisions as a matter of national citizenship.

Congressional debates in 1866 about the establishment of the Department of Education provide one clear example of how advocates tied calls for greater federal involvement in education to citizenship ideals.[26] Though the mission of the department, which quickly lost its cabinet status, was limited to data collection, debates about its creation revealed growing concern about federal responsibility for the quality of education that citizens receive, as well as the view that education is a right, as one member of Congress put it:

> I take the high ground that every child of this land is, by natural right, entitled to an education . . . and that this ought not to be left to the caprice of individuals or of States. . . . At least every child in the land should receive a sufficient education to qualify him to discharge all the duties that may devolve upon him as an American citizen. This is as much a natural right as the right to breathe the air and to be provided with food and clothing.[27]

The purpose of the Department of Education—to "enforce education, without regard to race or color, upon the population of all such States as shall fall below a standard to be established by Congress"—conveyed an educational threshold for equal citizenship, and aimed to compel Southern states to extend educational opportunities to newly freed slaves.[28] Related efforts by the Radical Republican Charles Sumner to require states to provide free public education to all students as a condition for statehood did not succeed in Congress. Yet debates about such proposals furthered the idea that equal citizenship, bolstered by the 15th Amendment's grant of universal male suffrage, necessitates universal high-quality education that the federal government has an obligation to provide. As Goodwin Liu highlights, these proposals envisioned federal involvement in terms of ensuring a sufficient standard for education rather than demanding strict equalization, a point to which I return later in this chapter.

After the creation of the Department of Education came the Hoar Bill of 1870, which aimed to create a national system of compulsory education with federal funding. The Hoar Bill sought to use the heft of the national government to compel states to provide an adequate education by threatening federal takeover of subpar state systems, mainly in southern states.[29] But even Representative Hoar did not have much hope that his bill would pass, given myriad objections to the bureaucracy it would create and to the power it would give to federal officials, including oversight of curriculum and textbooks.[30] Though the Hoar Bill did not become law, its rhetoric showcases how reformers linked concern for education, citizenship, and political equality to press for greater federal support of public schools. Hoar viewed education as a right flowing directly from the 14th and 15th Amendments' guarantees of equal citizenship: "Among the fundamental civil rights of the citizen is, by logical necessity, included the right to receive a full, free, ample education from the Government."[31]

Next in the series of proposals to increase federal support for education came the Blair Bill, which was one of the most significant early proposals for a federal role in regulating educational quality. Introduced in 1882 and debated in the Senate until 1890, the Blair Bill proposed a national fund for education that would be divided among states on the basis of levels of illiteracy—a design implicitly concerned with interstate equality. The bill also required state spending to match federal contributions, mandated that states receiving federal funds educate all school-age children (but did not require integrated schools), and established basic curricular requirements. Although this bill met the same fate as the Hoar Bill, Senate debate about it brought into sharp focus the idea that the federal government has a constitutional duty to prepare citizens to exercise their political rights. In Senator Blair's words, the government "has imposed upon itself the duty of educating the people of the United States whenever for any cause those people are deficient in that degree of education which is essential to the discharge of their duties as citizens."[32]

Although these attempts to legislate federal responsibility for education ended as noble failures, parallel attempts at the state level had greater success during Reconstruction. Most southern states did not guarantee access to public education in their constitutions prior to the Civil War. Under pressure from Congress, ten former Confederate states revised their constitutions between 1867 and 1870 to include provisions for education. These educational clauses vary widely from state to state; sometimes their language is vague and utopian, in other cases it is bureaucratic and technical. But the majority of state constitutions refer to education's central role in promoting democratic citizenship.[33] And despite the limited success of federal proposals during Reconstruction, reformers continued to press education as a national issue tied to political equality. The Great Depression over half a century later then forced the national perspective that earlier advocates sought. The widespread need for poverty relief could not be met by piecemeal state efforts, and New Deal aid programs reinvigorated the idea of education as a national right alongside entitlements to other social goods and opportunities.

THE NEW DEAL: RETHINKING RIGHTS, DUTIES, AND CONSTITUTIONAL MEANING

In 1944, Franklin Roosevelt outlined an ambitious new course for the country that aimed to pick up where the Constitution left off.[34] In his State of the Union address that wartime year, Roosevelt naturally focused on security. But he conveyed an expansive notion of security that stretched beyond concern about foreign enemies to include the domestic threat of poverty. Citizens' freedom and independence, emphasized Roosevelt, are contingent on security in this broader sense: "People who are hungry and out of a job are the stuff of which dictatorships are made."[35]

Roosevelt's view that the meaningful exercise of political liberties requires a certain degree of economic well-being not only increased federal involvement in social service provision. It also challenged the view that citizens are entitled only to political liberties (or negative rights), to the exclusion of welfare rights:

This Republic had its beginning, and grew to its present strength, under the protection of certain inalienable political rights—among them the right of free speech, free press, free worship, trial by jury, freedom from unreasonable searches and seizures. They were our rights to life and liberty. As our Nation has grown in size and stature, however—as our industrial economy expanded—these political rights proved inadequate to assure us equality in the pursuit of happiness. We have come to a clear realization of the fact that true individual freedom cannot exist without economic security and independence.[36]

Roosevelt's conviction that political rights alone would not ensure economic security motivated his proposal for an ambitious "Second Bill of Rights" that he introduced in this speech. Roosevelt did not advocate a constitutional amendment to recognize these rights; rather, he saw them as a statement of widespread commitment to economic security and equality that should be protected through democratic politics. They included the goods that welfare rights theorists typically focus on, such as employment, housing, and health care, with the notable addition of the "right to a good education" at the end of the list.[37]

The Second Bill of Rights and the New Deal programs preceding it have profoundly affected debates about citizenship, rights, and constitutional interpretation in the United States. Even though most of Roosevelt's proposals were never realized, they raise enduring questions about constitutional democracy and the scope of entitlements that flow from citizenship. These questions bear centrally on claims about educational rights, especially in terms of their legal viability.

Liberal legal scholars draw on Roosevelt's conception of rights to support welfare entitlements that go beyond the political liberties enumerated in the Constitution. Although proponents of this view commonly recognize the need for welfare rights as a matter of equal citizenship, they disagree about who should have the authority to legitimate rights claims. Some focus on the judiciary as the arbiter of rights, while others look to legislative bodies and popular opinion.[38] These debates are beyond my focus, but present-day arguments for welfare rights, mirroring Roosevelt's views, do provide justification for a right to education even though the Constitution does not say a word about education.

Consider Cass Sunstein's position that education is a "constitutive commitment."[39] Sunstein regards constitutive commitments as more enduring than particular policies but less entrenched than constitutional requirements: they "help to create, or constitute, a society's basic values" even though they are not constitutional rights.[40] The public's deeply entrenched expectation that the state provide all citizens with a good education, argues Sunstein, makes education a national commitment that carries the moral and political force of a right.

This view follows from Sunstein's belief that what we regard as a right need not be limited to what is explicitly recognized by the Constitution, because the Constitution, as we tend to interpret it, is partial in two ways. First, it treats the status quo as neutral; thus it is partial in the sense that it is biased toward current social and economic arrangements. Second, it is partial in the sense that it is incomplete because it is often understood as giving all interpretative authority to the courts.[41] Recognizing the partiality of the Constitution in these ways, argues Sunstein, opens up space for new rights that can be claimed and affirmed through the democratic process. The New Dealers, as Sunstein sees it, rightly used this space to press for change that was unlikely to come forth from courts.

This perspective suggests that education is a right that democratic bodies can realize even though it lacks the legal status of a federal constitutional right. But as I emphasize in chapter 1, democratic bodies are at best unreliable guardians of the rights of all students, and at worst they are the source of grave injustices. For these reasons, some argue, contra Sunstein, that a realistic appraisal of democratic politics justifies putting more faith in courts than in democratic politics to protect rights.[42] The ambiguous policy legacy of the New Deal is arguably a case in point. This period can be celebrated as a time when "we the people" aimed to reinterpret and expand constitutional rights without relying on the judiciary. Yet it is questionable whether the policies and programs from this period have an institutional legacy.[43] Roosevelt's Second Bill of Rights "fell with a dull thud into the half-empty chambers of the United States Congress," and none of its proposed entitlements are considered protected rights at the federal level today.[44]

Court-based education reform may institutionalize change when democratic politics come up short. The leading effort to date to win federal recognition of the right to education in court, however, was also a "noble failure." But it was a very close call. Although the U.S. Supreme Court's 5–4 decision in *San Antonio Independent School District v. Rodriguez* denied the existence of a federal right to education, it continues to leave its mark on legal and philosophical discourse about education entitlements.

THE *RODRIGUEZ* DECISION: EDUCATIONAL RIGHTS CLAIMS SENT BACK TO STATE COURTS

In 1968, a group of Mexican-American parents from the Edgewood Independent School District in San Antonio, Texas, sued the San Antonio School District over the vast funding inequalities among its districts. The plaintiffs' school district, one of seven in San Antonio, was the poorest in the region. Its schools spent $356 per pupil per year while the wealthiest district in the area, Alamo Heights, spent $594 per pupil, a difference that in today's dollars would be more than $1400.[45] And this funding disparity existed despite the fact that Edgewood had a higher property tax rate than Alamo Heights. Because property values in Edgewood were significantly lower than in Alamo Heights, Edgewood residents would have to tax themselves at a rate twenty times that of Alamo Heights to yield equal funds for education.[46] The plaintiffs argued that the funding disparity between these districts was unconstitutional and that the San Antonio district was culpable because of its reliance on property tax revenue to fund its schools.[47]

The U.S. Supreme Court's 1973 decision on this matter denied that the equal protection clause of the Fourteenth Amendment could be used to advance students' right to an equal education. This halted school finance litigation at the federal level. In reversing the lower court's decision, which supported the Edgewood parents, the Supreme Court refuted the parents' two central arguments. First, it found that the Edgewood students do not constitute a so-called "suspect class,"—that is, members of a group that has historically experienced discrimination—which would have placed a greater burden on the San Antonio district to defend its funding scheme.[48] Second, the Court found that education is not a fundamental right under the federal Constitution. To arrive at its decision, the majority adopted an uncharitable interpretation of the parents' claims. It is important to understand the claims that animated the parents' case, which almost won federal recognition of the right to education.[49]

The Logic of the Parents' Case

The *Rodriguez* case was fueled by parents' moral outrage about their children's relative educational disadvantage. Why should less money be spent on the education of Edgewood students simply because their parents live in less expensive housing? This foundational moral concern was translated into a legal argument with the help of ideas from the 1970 book *Private Wealth and Public Education*, by John Coons, William Clune, and Stephen

Sugarman.[50] In this book, Coons and his colleagues reported findings on the correlation between educational inputs (money) and outputs (student achievement). They concluded that the quality of the education children receive should not depend on the wealth of the school district in which they happen to reside. Their reasoning became the backbone of the Edgewood parents' legal strategy.[51]

Coons and his colleagues argued that relying on property taxes to fund education amounts to de facto discrimination against children in property-poor districts. The state is especially culpable for inequalities in education, they insisted, because of its hand in designing the system that produces these inequalities. Whereas the disadvantages associated with poverty (such as poor health and inadequate housing) "are not the anticipated consequence of government planning," nothing other than educational inequality could be expected from a system that, by design, ties schooling opportunities to wealth.[52] This line of argument enabled the Edgewood plaintiffs to use the equal protection clause of the Fourteenth Amendment to advance their case for funding equality, which was a legal strategy that had recently worked for poor plaintiffs who had challenged inequalities in other policy areas.[53]

Equal protection discourse was central to *Rodriguez*, but the parents' case was also grounded in the contrary logic of adequacy claims. After all, the central point in the *Rodriguez* case was that inequalities in educational opportunity in particular are especially troubling, not unequal opportunities in general. Legal scholar Peter Edelman underscores this point by comparing access to education to access to the municipal opera.[54] Clearly, access to the opera based on ability to pay is less morally troubling than access to education based on wealth; this suggests that something more than concerns about equality influences our view of educational justice. Frank Michelman makes the same point by comparing education to golf.[55] If we really care about minimizing the effects of poverty, he argues, then equality cannot be our only concern, because equality can be realized by making everyone equally impoverished. What matters more than an equal distribution of resources is ensuring that all citizens have an adequate amount of what they need. The adequacy perspective compels us to distinguish between more and less fundamental goods and opportunities because it "reacts more hospitably than evenhandedness to the question: why education and not golf?"[56]

The *Rodriguez* case thus turned on the question of whether education, because of its particular influence on individuals' lives, warrants the status of a fundamental right. The Edgewood parents' lawyers argued that education is distinct from other public services because of its special connection to political rights enumerated in the Constitution, namely the right to free speech and the right to vote. Their claim was that the meaningful exercise of voting and free speech rights depends on a certain degree of knowledge and skill:

> While, no doubt, the First Amendment protects uninformed, unper-suasive, and possibly unintelligible speech, the meaningful exercise of that right, enabling the speaker to convince and persuade, is dependent upon his ability to speak intelligently and knowledgeably. This is the es-sence of free speech guarantee. It is not the act of vocalizing meaningless sounds that is the raison d'être for judicial protection; rather it is the pro-cess of exchanging ideas for the purpose of gaining 'wisdom in action.'[57]

In their insistence on this connection between knowledge and effective political participation, Edgewood parents did not argue that it is the state's responsibility to enable citizens to make maximum use of their political rights via education. Yet the Court's majority wrongly ascribed that more extreme position to the plaintiffs when ruling against their claims.

The Supreme Court's Response: Polarizing Options for Judicial Redress

The Supreme Court's majority opinion did not contest the parents' claim that there is a special connection between education and the exercise of political liberties. It summarized the plaintiffs' arguments on this point and expressed its agreement: "They insist that education is itself a fundamen-tal personal right because it is essential to the effective exercise of First Amendment freedoms and to intelligent utilization of the right to vote. . . . We need not dispute any of these propositions."[58] What the Court majority did challenge, however, is the claim that the Texas school funding system denied students the "basic minimal skills" necessary for effective political participation.[59] The opinion recognized that some amount of education is necessary to make other rights meaningful—a point that opens the door to recognition of a minimal right to education, as subsequent cases citing *Rodriguez* have argued.[60] Yet the majority found that Texas surely provided that minimum, and thus avoided any substantive discussion of what this minimal right might entail.

Moreover, the majority expressed concern about having to recognize a host of other welfare rights should it grant education the status of a right. Even if some amount of education is crucial to the meaningful exercise of constitutionally protected political liberties, the majority wrote, where can we draw the line? "The logical limitations on appellees' nexus theory are difficult to perceive," the opinion reads. "How, for instance, is education to be distinguished from the significant personal interest in the basics of decent food and shelter?"[61]

The Court was not convinced that education is the most important social good for realizing citizens' political liberties. The majority also argued that the Court could not guarantee citizens the most effective use of free speech rights or the most informed choice at the polls[62]—even though Edgewood parents did not claim that the state is obligated to enable citizens to make maximum use of their rights via education.[63] The Court misconstrued parents' claims into this superlative form even though this maximizing standard was not necessary for recognition of a federal right to education.

By extension, the Court also unnecessarily limited its options for describing the state's obligation to provide for education to one of two choices: to find that the state is responsible for providing an education that enables the most effective free speech or electoral choices, or to find that any state effort at providing education is sufficient. Given the impossibility of realizing the former maximizing standard, the Court endorsed the anemic latter option. This choice unnecessarily foreclosed any substantive discussion of what counts as a satisfactory minimal education and ignored the possibilities between these extremes that could improve opportunities for Edgewood students.

Similarly, the majority expressed an unnecessarily polarized way of thinking about the Court's obligation to remedy the inequalities that the Edgewood parents presented. Their opinion conveyed that judicial redress is warranted only when citizens are completely denied benefits like public education, rather than in instances of inadequate or unequal educational opportunities.[64] Finally, because education is not a right explicitly mentioned in the Constitution, the majority argued that the Texas financing system did not warrant the strictest level of judicial scrutiny. It argued that the weaker "rational basis" test applied, which simply required Texas to prove that its financing system was rationally related to a state interest. By applying this standard, the majority found that the state's interest in protecting local control of education was reason enough to condone its school funding system.

MARSHALL'S DISSENT AND THE NEXUS THEORY

Justice Marshall's dissenting opinion offers a more sensitive approach to the morally complex problems presented in the *Rodriguez* case. I disagree with his reasoning, though, on the question of whether a right to education necessitates an equity or adequacy model for distributing resources. Marshall's much-quoted dissent departed from the majority's opinion on both central points: he affirmed that the students in the Edgewood district should count as a suspect class because they had suffered wealth-based discrimination, and he agreed with the parents that education is a fundamental right. His reasoning on both matters is motivated by his view of "the right of every American to an equal start in life."[65] The idea that it is the state's responsibility to provide citizens with an equal opportunity for economic and social mobility via education, at least when they are young, echoes Roosevelt's concern about the material preconditions to the meaningful exercise of political rights, and presents a very different approach from the Court majority's view of the relationship between citizenship, education, and equality.

Although the majority did not deny that preparing students to exercise their political liberties is a constitutionally relevant concern, Marshall's recognition of the relationship between education and political participation is more forceful and unequivocal: "Education directly affects the ability of a child to exercise his First Amendment rights, both as a source and as a receiver of information and ideas, whatever interests he may pursue in life."[66] Marshall argued that education is a fundamental right because of its strong correlation with the exercise of political liberties, a view that put him at odds with the majority in terms of the appropriate standard for judicial review of the Texas financing system. Standards for review should not be as black and white as the majority suggested, Marshall argued, because citizens' ability to use their enumerated liberties effectively may require the protection of unenumerated rights like education.[67] Marshall therefore argued for the appropriateness of a spectrum of review standards that takes into account how close or distant the issue at hand is to an enumerated constitutional right.[68]

Given the tight link between education and enumerated political liberties, Marshall argued that a stringent review standard was justified in this case. Meeting this heightened standard, known as "strict scrutiny," would require Texas to demonstrate that its school financing system serves a compelling state interest and is the least restrictive way of realizing that interest. Such a review, Marshall concluded, could not possibly condone the Texas financing system. Marshall recognized the value of local control of education but argued that in this case it served "as an excuse rather than as a justification for interdistrict inequality."[69]

Much ink has been spilled about the important legal issues at hand here, including standards for judicial review, what counts as a suspect class, and how we should interpret the equal protection clause. I want to set aside these legal concerns to take up a critically important philosophical question that Marshall's dissent raises, and that continues to animate policy debates about educational rights today: Should educational resources be distributed on an equal basis or according to an adequacy threshold? Marshall sided with equality and rejected the idea of a constitutional minimum for education, in part because he deemed an adequacy standard to be too complex for courts to define and enforce.[70] Yet when we look beyond this pragmatic concern about judicial enforcement, it is not clear that an equality standard is better able to realize the ideal of equal citizenship than the adequacy approach.

MOVING AHEAD: THE ADEQUACY APPROACH TO THE RIGHT TO EDUCATION

Political theorists engaged in the debate between equity and adequacy disagree about whether all inequalities among schools should be condemned as injustices, or whether an adequacy threshold that tolerates inequalities above it is acceptable. A sticking point between the two sides of this debate centers on the nature of education's value, and on how that should influence the distribution of educational resources. Proponents of equality like William Koski and Rob Reich emphasize the positional attributes of education. Education is a positional good, they argue, because its value is not absolute; rather, as they see it, the value of my education is relative to the quality and quantity of your education, and because the field is a competitive one, educational resources should be distributed equally.[71]

Proponents of adequacy may not dispute the positionality of education, but they do not think that this should dictate how resources are divided. They argue that the demand for equality as opposed to adequacy is rooted in envy of some parents' freedom to invest in their children's education above the adequacy threshold as they see fit.[72] Since their position is construed as morally less demanding, proponents of adequacy are usually on the defensive in this debate and have to refute the criticism that their view betrays the ideal of equal educational opportunity.

When this debate focuses on the private and economic returns to education, I agree that adequacy proponents have a harder case to make. As Koski and Reich illustrate, the fierce competition for coveted slots at elite colleges and universities is evidence enough of education's positionality in the economic realm. Research clearly demonstrates that students who attend selective universities disproportionately attended private high schools, and their advantages will continue to accrue because of the economic benefits of earning a college diploma at a highly selective institution.[73] In light of the significant advantages that come from having more education, and a more elite education, adequacy is a tough case to make.

In defense of their view, adequacy proponents like Elizabeth Anderson and Debra Satz point to the fact that educational inequalities may work to the advantage of the least well-off. If the total economic pie is enlarged by the talents of those who receive a superior education, then relative deprivation should not matter much since the least well-off benefit from the economic, social, and intellectual achievements of the educational elite. As Anderson puts it, "No one is entitled to demand a smaller pie, just so that they can get a larger proportional slice."[74] Egalitarians find this argument unconvincing because it condones the "dignitary harms" that follow from educational inequalities. Some argue further that the benefits that privileged students accrue are unlikely to redound to the benefit of the less advantaged.[75] And even if some benefits do trickle down, they may not be great enough to compensate less advantaged students for their compromised position in college admissions and in the labor market.[76]

Yet when this debate focuses on civic rather than economic returns to education, it is less obvious that education is significantly positional and that the egalitarians have the stronger argument. To be sure, there are some features of education that yield positional political advantages. Those with a superior education might be better at detecting truth and fallacy in public discourse. They may be able to deliver better arguments to advance their positions, and they may be able to avoid manipulation more easily. However, there are other aspects of political influence that do not follow exclusively, or even largely, from formal education. The personal assets that give one influence in the public sphere—such as displaying confidence and being able to establish rapport with others—may have as much to do with non-academic skills as they do with formal academic training. In public deliberations, a Harvard graduate who is socially ill-at-ease may have no advantage over a charismatic high school drop-out.

Similarly, some of the economic advantages that follow from an elite education do not necessarily translate into political advantages. Although graduates of elite institutions may have higher average incomes, their financial advantages could (at least in theory) be neutralized in the political sphere by campaign finance regulations. In addition, advocacy organizations like the one I consider in chapter 5 can provide political training to marginalized citizens that enables them to advocate for their interests on equal footing with their better-educated compatriots.

Yet these possibilities do not negate the tight correlation between formal education and political equality, or the importance of policies that take this connection seriously. That education is less positional in the civic than in the economic realm hardly means that it is unimportant to the effective exercise of political liberties.

The adequacy framework is the better approach for thinking about civic education because it demands a substantive focus on the content of that education. It is also less vulnerable to significant challenges that the equity model faces, including steep political resistance and concerns about leveling down to achieve equality. Yet as some adequacy proponents have rightly suggested, we need not think about these two approaches to educational distribution in such a starkly dichotomous way.

Satz's conception of educational adequacy, for example, incorporates both egalitarian and comparative concerns. She emphasizes that the minimum educational threshold for achieving civic equality depends on the knowledge and skills others have, so it is a moving target.[77] Liu similarly argues that the specifics of an adequacy threshold must be tailored to particular contexts, which includes attention to levels of inequality in a society: "adequacy is not distinct from, but rather informed by, the conditions of inequality in a given social context."[78] Satz and Anderson also rightly emphasize that education for equal citizenship requires attention to how students are distributed among schools because class and race segregation prevents social mobility and cross-group understanding.[79] A morally compelling conception of adequacy does not demand an equal distribution of education resources, but it does insist that students attend schools that are integrated as a matter of civic equality. This approach better promotes equal citizenship than a focus on the equalization of educational resources, which in practice is often reduced to a question of funding.

In sum, more and better education does not necessarily confer political advantages even if it does confer economic advantages. The link between educational opportunity and political influence is far looser, which justifies the adequacy approach over the equity one. Yet civic competence is hardly noncomparative; any adequacy threshold must be sensitive to changing social and political expectations. Furthermore, the equity and adequacy approaches to educational opportunity can work in tandem. Once citizens have the civic skills to participate in public discourse effectively, then they can engage in public deliberations about economic and other policies that may improve their conditions.

I have highlighted key moments in U.S. history during which the executive, legislative, or judicial branch of government considered—and, in the case of *Rodriguez*, came quite close to endorsing—a right to education to advance equal citizenship. These moments illustrate not only the endurance of rights-based arguments for education reform, but also how such arguments have been animated by concern for realizing the ideals of deliberative citizenship. There are myriad countervailing historical moments and currents of thought. Nonetheless, the examples in this chapter illustrate that theoretical arguments for a right to education have historical traction.

These historical debates may also offer guidance for how to proceed today, especially as rights claims about education reform enjoy a resurgence in political discourse. Echoing earlier reformers, the current Secretary of Education, Arne Duncan, has repeatedly proclaimed education to be "the civil rights issue of our generation," while other education advocates have lobbied for a constitutional amendment that would make education a federal right.[80]

How could such a right be realized today in law, or more broadly as a constitutive commitment? In the second part of this book I turn to this pragmatic question. I begin by considering educational rights claims as they are invoked in their most common context: legal advocacy. Although there is a strong moral rationale for federal recognition of a right to education, the reality of the *Rodriguez* decision necessitates a state-by-state approach to litigation. The lawsuit I turn to next is therefore situated at the state level.

PART 2

Educational Rights in Practice

CHAPTER FOUR

The *Rose* Case: A Case Study
in Legal Advocacy

We educate our children here to make intelligent voters of them. . . .
The main object of our public schools is that our young people may be
intelligent enough to exercise the right of suffrage.
—William M. Beckner[1]

Kentucky has the most illiterate citizenry in the country and the highest
percentage of counties with undereducated populations. In Kentucky, 46
counties—roughly 40%—have the lowest possible average educational
attainment among their citizens.
—Brief for Appellees, *Rose v. Council for Better Education*[2]

My analysis so far has focused on making the philosophical case for a
right to education as a matter of political equality. In the preceding
chapters I argue that a right to education is a necessary precondition for deliberative democracy, sketched out what this right should entail, and highlighted the historical precedents for rooting this right in the ideal of equal
citizenship in the United States. In part 2 I focus on how students' right to
education for equal citizenship can be realized, given prevailing political,
institutional, and legal conditions.

In this chapter and the next I offer empirical case studies of two different
but related strategies for instituting a right to education: school resource
litigation at the state level, and community-based organizing at the local
level. These two types of advocacy are at the forefront of education reform
efforts and have a significant presence across the United States. Over five
hundred community organizing groups across the country are estimated to
be engaged in education reform, while lawyers have challenged school funding systems in forty-five states to date.[3]

And most important for my analysis, both reform strategies are centrally motivated by rights claims. Community groups rally around the claim that math proficiency and literacy are civil rights, for example, in order to hold public officials accountable for school conditions. Meanwhile, litigators aim to protect and expand students' legal right to a quality education via judicial review. Taken together, these reform strategies provide an opportunity to observe rights claims at work in both communities and courtrooms as they are expressed by various actors, including community organizers, school officials, parents, students, and lawyers.

The case studies that follow highlight the challenges advocates face as they work to institutionalize students' right to education. My focus on the actual conditions that advocates confront is a departure from the philosophical focus of earlier chapters. Case studies are necessarily context-specific, so the lessons they offer are not as general as the theoretical arguments I advanced in part 1. However, connecting theory to practice is important for any political philosophy that aims to be meaningful in the real world, especially when it comes to analysis of rights. This is because of the hybrid nature of rights claims: they are moral, political, philosophical, and strategic statements. Their multifaceted character is demonstrated by philosophers' ongoing interest in rights, as well as by rights' prominence in today's pressing policy debates. As philosopher and legal scholar Jeremy Waldron put it, because rights are a matter of political and not just moral philosophy, we must be attentive to how they cohere with the "institutional arrangements of human society."[4]

In this spirit, the case studies that follow showcase how moral claims about a right to education might be translated into democratic activism and public policy in the United States. What moral and political force do claims about a right to education have in courtrooms and communities? And what can these claims accomplish toward realizing better educational opportunities for students? In this chapter I begin to answer these questions by considering how a landmark lawsuit in Kentucky, *Rose v. Council for Better Education*, affirmed students' right to education in that state and prompted sweeping policy changes.[5] In the next chapter I examine the ways in which a leading child advocacy organization in San Francisco employs rights discourse in its education reform efforts, and to what effect. Although these two types of advocacy represent distinct approaches to reform, they can intersect in mutually reinforcing ways. In the concluding chapter I consider how lawyers and community groups can collaborate to realize students' right to education, and the democratic value of these collaborations toward advancing civic dialogue about education reform in the United States.

A CHALLENGE TO EDUCATIONAL INEQUALITIES
AND INADEQUACIES IN KENTUCKY

In the spring of 1984, the striking gap in Kentucky between schools' lofty goals and woeful outcomes drove Arnold Guess to action. As a former Kentucky Department of Education employee, Guess knew well the inadequacies of the state's education system, and he had decided that it was time to leverage the law for reform.[6] In a memo appealing to superintendents across the state, he wrote: "It appears that all remedies have been exhausted except testing the question before our state courts."[7]

The question at hand was: Had the Kentucky General Assembly met its constitutional obligation to provide students a quality education? Key measures of educational achievement strongly suggested that it had not. Among U.S. states, Kentucky had the lowest percentage of adults over age twenty-five with a high school diploma and one of the lowest per-pupil expenditure levels (43rd in the country). Educational outcomes were especially dismal in Kentucky's Appalachian districts, where almost half the population was functionally illiterate.[8] A common refrain in the state was "Thank God for Mississippi" because Mississippi spared Kentucky from holding last place in national education rankings.[9]

Guess's call for action quickly gained support from district leaders across the state. Although superintendents served as the primary plaintiffs in the subsequent litigation, growing and broad-based public demand for school reform softened the political context for the sweeping court decision that was to come. Without broad public support, the case, *Rose v. Council for Better Education*, might have had a different, or at least less dramatic, outcome. The court's unprecedented decision—that the state's entire educational system was unconstitutional and that students have a right to education that prepares them for citizenship and the labor market—was the payoff for public mobilization as well as careful legal strategy. The scope of the decision surprised even the plaintiffs' lead litigator, who said of the outcome: "We expected a thimbleful and we got a bucketful."[10]

Conditions in Kentucky were unique in many ways, but a number of other state courts have borrowed heavily from *Rose*, giving it a legacy that reaches across the United States.[11] Moreover, the case is often celebrated as the beginning of the "third wave" of school finance litigation, in which plaintiffs shifted their focus from equity to adequacy claims, yielding a greater success rate in court.[12] Although the *Rose* case is now over two decades old, its genesis and outcomes hold important lessons for ongoing school finance reform and our evolving conception of what a legal right to education entails.

A significant but underanalyzed feature of cases like *Rose* is how moral claims about educational entitlements can facilitate legal mobilization. To be sure, moral claims are usually far more expansive than what courts recognize, and the gap between what the best political morality recommends and what the judiciary will recognize understandably divides most analysis of education litigation. Philosophers who write about particular cases are largely concerned with the rights that students should have, while legal scholars tend to focus on rights that positive law can support. But this division of labor overlooks an important dimension of *Rose* and other school finance cases: how moral claims can inspire citizens to mobilize and support litigation, which in turn can affect judicial outcomes and policy implementation.

Drawing upon legal documents filed with the court, advocates' reports, and interviews with litigators, reformers, and public officials, I examine how particular educational rights claims figured into the *Rose* case, and where they converged with and diverged from moral claims about educational justice. This focus highlights the interplay between moral and legal conceptions of educational rights, and how philosophical ideals about a right to education that I advanced in the first part of the book may shape rights-based advocacy in the United States.

"NAMING, BLAMING, AND CLAIMING"
TO BUILD THE KENTUCKY CASE

The year 1984 was an eventful one for the budding litigation effort that would transform Kentucky schools. The group of superintendents that Guess convened formed an advocacy group, the Council for Better Education, which held its first meeting in May with representatives from twenty-eight districts across the state. School finance experts presented funding data and discussed possible legal action with the group, which decided without dissent to proceed with a lawsuit.[13] Two of Guess's longtime friends, school finance expert Kern Alexander and attorney Theodore Lavit, contributed their expertise and were instrumental in shaping the legal complaint that would follow.

By October 1984, the Council for Better Education had secured additional legal representation by a renowned Kentucky public figure, Bert Combs, a former governor and former federal judge then in private practice. Combs made it clear that he was not keen to take on the case: "As a name partner in one of Kentucky's largest law firms, I needed to sue the Governor and the General Assembly about as much as a hog needs a side saddle."[14]

But Guess persisted and Combs finally agreed, and his political stature gave the plaintiffs "instant credibility."[15]

On a separate but related front, a citizens advocacy group that had formed in 1983 was reaching a broad base of Kentuckians and tapping into their growing discontent with public schools. Called the Prichard Committee for Academic Excellence, the group grew out of a commission appointed by the governor to review higher education in Kentucky. The commission had come to the conclusion that problems in postsecondary education had deep roots in the K–12 system, so it reorganized as an advocacy organization to address those issues.[16]

The Prichard Committee benefited from the involvement of some of Kentucky's most prominent business leaders and public servants, including its first director, Edward Prichard Jr. a native Kentuckian who had clerked for Supreme Court justice Felix Frankfurter and had been part of Franklin Roosevelt's New Deal "brain trust."[17] It also quickly engaged a broader base of citizens, most notably in televised town hall forums it organized in the fall of 1984. On a single evening in October of that year, almost 20,000 individuals gathered in venues across the state to address the question: "What do you want your schools to do?" These forums helped focus citizens' concerns and sent a clear message to elected officials that an engaged public expected change.[18] A special legislative session following this event failed to reform the state's school finance system, so the Council for Better Education filed its legal complaint in district court in November 1985.

Although a growing movement for reform certainly bolstered the nascent lawsuit, the plaintiffs faced significant obstacles in both the courtroom and the court of public opinion. Data on the inequalities and inadequacies of Kentucky schools would not alone compel change; litigators had to decide how they would frame these numbers. Furthermore, the Supreme Court's *Rodriguez* decision had closed the door on certain federal claims about a right to education, so the litigators made the Kentucky Constitution their focus.

The Council for Better Education was also keenly aware of the need to avoid strategies for redressing inequalities that might be seen as Robin Hood attempts, whereby poorer districts would gain funding at the expense of wealthier districts. Although there was reportedly "no such thing as a rich district" in Kentucky, the plaintiffs knew that it would be politically important to win the support of, or at least avoid opposition from, more affluent districts.[19] They succeeded on this front by getting superintendents from 66 of the state's 180 districts to serve as named plaintiffs, including district leaders from some of the state's wealthier areas. The state's demographics facilitated this unity: because Kentucky has a relatively homogeneous population, racial politics were kept at bay and the urban/rural comparison was more salient. As one observer put it, "The issue wasn't we're doing a good job for our white kids and a bad job for black kids. The issue really was we're doing a good job for our city kids and a lousy job for our country kids."[20] Moreover, since none of the districts had enough money, even the better-funded urban districts, the plaintiffs' driving message that everyone stood to gain from the litigation was a compelling one.

Another type of challenge arose as advocates worked to galvanize broader public support for their reform movement. Whatever merit legal claims might have in court, some Kentuckians were not convinced that reform was necessary or would be beneficial to them. Some parents "felt like what was good enough for them was good enough for their children," and they worried that greater educational opportunity would prompt their children to move away in pursuit of better career possibilities.[21] As a former state official put it, some parents didn't want their children to become "so well-educated that the next county can't hold them."[22]

To overcome these sorts of obstacles, education reformers often have to instigate a shift in how individuals perceive their routine experiences with schools. What may have been normal features of daily life (for example, dilapidated school facilities, low achievement, limited job prospects)—perhaps across generations—must come to be seen as morally egregious. This requisite shift in perspective has been described as "naming, blaming, and claiming," a process in which individuals reinterpret their experiences as unjust, identify a responsible party, and stake a claim to better treatment.[23]

Though this process may seem simple enough to initiate, requiring only that individuals recognize they have been wronged, it is riddled with difficulties that scholars of law and social movements have analyzed.[24] One fundamental problem in cases like *Rose* is that parents and students whose schooling experiences are limited to severely underresourced schools may understandably have low expectations for what a good education entails. This is the problem of the "acquiescence of the oppressed": individuals acclimate to conditions that outsiders would regard as severe deprivation.[25] This challenge is compounded by the funding structure for public schools in Kentucky and most other states. Because local property taxes are a significant determinant of school quality, families in property-poor areas may have little or no exposure to what better-funded schools can offer.

It is a moral rather than a legal sense of justice that prompts most people to rethink their experiences and to feel entitled to better conditions. As Jack

Moreland, president of the Council for Better Education during *Rose*, commented, "I don't think the rank-and-file person, and maybe even the rank-and-file superintendent, knew and understood the legal side of it. I do think that most people felt like we had a moral responsibility to the kids that were not getting a quality education."[26] As cases like *Rose* take shape, moral conceptions of educational justice play a critical role that facts and legal claims usually cannot accomplish on their own. What inspired most parents and district leaders and some public officials to support the litigation was not their estimation of the constitutional claims at hand, but rather concern for "the fundamental question of fairness" and a conviction that children's opportunities should not be dictated by the morally arbitrary circumstances into which they are born and raised.[27]

Moral ideas about students' right to education were propagated and sustained by several sources as the *Rose* case unfolded. The media played a huge role in increasing public awareness of schools' deficiencies and raising expectations for better opportunities. The state's three major newspapers ran articles exposing problems ranging from eye-catching issues like badly deteriorating school facilities to more abstract concerns, such as intradistrict spending disparities. The Louisville *Courier-Journal* ran a number of articles about corruption in eastern Kentucky school districts, while the *Lexington Herald-Leader* printed a series, titled "Cheating Our Children," that highlighted how low property tax assessments were starving schools.[28]

Parents' testimony in public forums organized by the Prichard Committee and other advocates was also influential in calling attention, in more personal ways, to the moral harm done when children receive an inadequate education. Cindy Heine, associate director of the Prichard Committee, recalled one parent's poignant testimony at a public event she organized in Lexington: "'I got outta high school and I wasn't able to read. I want something better for my children.' Of course, that got us all choked up and was very compelling."[29] Site visits to schools also provided compelling evidence of the dire need for change; former state senator David Karem remembered visiting a science classroom in eastern Kentucky that had pre–World War II encyclopedias and an out-of-date periodic table. "People were becoming horrified by that," he said.[30]

That sense of horror was essential for galvanizing and maintaining public support for *Rose*. Advocates had to upend citizens' acquiescence about school conditions—most importantly for those with children attending woefully inadequate schools, but ideally for a broader base of citizens, too. Moral claims typically have far more traction at this stage of the legal process than claims about legal entitlements. By appealing to citizens' intuitions about right and wrong, moral claims can throw into sharp relief unjust conditions and empower individuals to "name, blame, and claim" in pursuit of better opportunities.

Although the *Rose* plaintiffs were primarily superintendents rather than individual parents or students, the sense of injustice and moral outrage that came to characterize the public's opinion of school conditions was critical to the political success of court-based reform.[31] The Prichard Committee's role on this front was crucial; its education and outreach efforts served as the "galvanizing force to make the state recognize the moral imperative and practical necessity of improving its schools."[32] Yet the next step in the litigation process, crafting arguments that will have standing in court, necessarily brought legal claims to the fore and exposed potential gaps between moral and legal understandings of educational rights.

ADEQUACY, EQUITY, AND EFFICIENCY IN *ROSE*

The Council for Better Education's legal complaint, filed with the trial court in November 1985, centered on a seemingly straightforward claim: that Section 183 of the Kentucky Constitution holds the state's General Assembly responsible for providing an "efficient" system of public schools, and that this duty had been flagrantly neglected. Yet what *efficient* means in this context is far from clear; the Kentucky Constitution does not define the term when describing the state's educational obligation.[33] Moreover, although the state assembly is explicitly required by the state's Constitution to maintain the public school system, the plaintiffs' decision to name as defendants the governor, superintendent of public schools, state treasurer, and leaders of both houses of the General Assembly was hardly uncontroversial.[34] As Combs's co-counsel Debra Dawahare put it, since the Kentucky Constitution (like most state constitutions) did not provide much detail about the nature and scope of students' educational entitlements, it offered "either very sparse language or very spacious language depending on how you wanted to look at it. And we decided to look at it as spacious."[35] Given this interpretive leeway in framing the case, plaintiffs strategically made decisions in view of achievement and funding data, legal precedent, and the political viability of arguments they might press.

In addition to local conditions that shaped the framing of *Rose*, almost two decades of school finance litigation across the United States also influenced the Council for Better Education's plan. As legal scholars have written about at length, and as I discuss in chapter 3, many observers of school finance reform emphasize that there are two competing approaches to litigation, equity and adequacy.[36] The equity approach is comparative and addresses differences across schools or districts, whereas the adequacy approach is noncomparative and focuses on absolute deprivation—that is, whether school conditions fall below a minimum threshold. *Rose* is celebrated for ushering in the adequacy approach and for prompting advocates in other states to follow the same approach.

The *Rose* plaintiffs employed the adequacy approach in view of litigation outcomes in other states, and because local factors made claims about absolute deprivation more viable than claims strictly focused on equity. Most notably, the Council for Better Education's attorneys and advisors had watched closely as California's *Serrano* decision unfolded in the 1970s. *Serrano* focused on equity claims and resulted in a landmark decision that equalized school funding across the state.[37] There were certainly disparities among Kentucky districts, but the situation was very different there. As Richard Salmon, one of the plaintiffs' finance experts, put it, there was "equalized poverty" in Kentucky because no district had enough resources: "They're all poor," he said.[38] Moreover, the equity approach had recently resulted in courtroom losses for plaintiffs in a number of states; by 1988, plaintiffs had won only 7 of the 22 equity cases heard by state supreme courts.[39] This reality, coupled with the questionable political viability of equity claims in Kentucky, made adequacy a more promising path. But it required careful consideration of what specific claims would gain traction in court and entailed setting aside certain arguments about educational justice.

Claims about absolute rather than relative deprivation may have been politically expedient, but on what legal basis were these claims made, and to what effect? What trade-offs were involved with respect to moral ideals about students' entitlements? First, it is important to note that the plaintiffs did not drop equity concerns altogether. Their complaint does highlight how educational disparities followed from the varying fiscal capacity of school districts resulting from different property values and tax rates. While the wealthiest school district in Kentucky at the time of *Rose* had assessed property per pupil valued at $259,675, the poorest district had just $28,745.[40] Moreover as the plaintiffs' complaint contends, state contributions to local efforts failed to compensate for these disparities, resulting in lower teacher pay, higher dropout rates, fewer course offerings, and lower achievement for students in poorer schools.[41] From an equity standpoint, the plaintiffs' attorneys argued that these disparities violated the Kentucky Constitution's call for "an efficient system of common schools," as well as the federal equal protection clause of the Fourteenth Amendment.[42]

Although the Council for Better Education initially focused on the relative deprivation of Kentucky's poorer districts, it did not focus exclusively on inequalities. The novel step in their complaint was to invoke adequacy claims as part and parcel of what an efficient public school system requires. Although the Kentucky Constitution does not offer a definition of *efficient*, the plaintiffs tied efficiency to adequacy by arguing that under state statutes "there exists an official conception of an 'adequate/efficient' public school curriculum . . . [that] reflects national as well as state-wide values and practices."[43] Plaintiffs' attorneys pressed this claim to avoid resting their case exclusively on controversial equity arguments and to underscore that all Kentucky schools—especially in view of national averages—were subpar. As Salmon put it, "We took the word 'efficient' and we really rode that horse as far as we could."[44]

That horse carried them quite far with both the trial court and the Kentucky Supreme Court. The trial court's sweeping decision, issued by Judge Ray Corns on May 31, 1988, emphatically supported the plaintiffs' view of what an efficient education entails. It was a stroke of luck that Corns was assigned to hear the case, given his background and sympathy with reformers' cause. He had previously been chief counsel for the Kentucky Department of Education and had authored a casebook on education law with plaintiffs' consultant Alexander.[45]

In his decision, Corns wrote that *efficient* is a "term of art" in the education realm and that its meaning extends beyond the economic sense to require that the state's public education be "adequate, uniform, and unitary."[46] Corns also affirmed that education is a fundamental right under the Kentucky Constitution, and he appointed a select committee, chaired by Alexander, to review data and propose remedies to realize this right. Although Corns did not explicitly propose a tax increase, this was implied given his conclusion that no district was "so affluent that it would justify having their present level of funding diminished."[47]

In its report to Judge Corns, the select committee detailed the meaning of key terms from the Kentucky Constitution that the case rested on, including *efficient, common schools, a system of schools*, and most notably, *adequate*. With respect to adequacy, the committee wrote philosophically of the significance of an adequate education to "the needs of individuals and society," and it presented five criteria for determining whether the adequacy standard has been met.[48] In his final judgment, Corns adopted and elaborated these ambitious criteria, which span individual, economic, cultural, and most important for my purposes, citizenship goals for education.[49]

Although Corns deferred to legislators the task of devising a remedy for the problems the case highlighted, some defendants believed that the state's separation of powers doctrine had been violated.[50] The governor chose not to contest the decision, but the leaders of the House and the Senate, Donald J. Blandford and John A. Rose, respectively, quickly filed an appeal. The state supreme court agreed to hear their appeal immediately, and the case assumed Rose's name, becoming known as *Rose v. Council for Better Education.*

At the next stage of litigation, the appellants focused on technical aspects of the case, such as whether the plaintiffs had standing and whether the trial court had violated Kentucky's separation of powers doctrine. In response, Bert Combs remained focused on more substantive issues. He presented data on funding inequalities and inadequacies, and he appealed to state pride and pressed the moral rationale for reform: "Kentucky has become recognized, unfortunately, as the most illiterate state in the nation. . . . Countless young minds throughout our fair state are being wasted."[51] In the end, Combs's data and moral arguments prevailed. The Kentucky Supreme Court's 5–2 decision, issued in June of 1989, went above and beyond the already dramatic trial court decision. Writing for the majority, Chief Justice Stephens surprisingly and unequivocally declared that the entire system of public education in Kentucky was unconstitutional: "There is no allegation that only part of the common school system is invalid. . . . This decision applies to the entire sweep of the system—all its parts and parcels."[52] Such resolute language is present throughout the decision, which squarely sides with the Council for Better Education in affirming the legitimacy of their claims, the strength of their evidence (which the Court wrote "literally engulfs that of the appellants"), and the dire need for change because the importance of education "cannot be overemphasized or understated."[53]

Most notably, the court endorsed a right to education that centers on equal access to an adequate education, writing that "Each child, every child, in this Commonwealth must be provided with an equal opportunity to have an adequate education."[54] This strong statement of students' entitlements was heralded by reform advocates as an unprecedented victory that went far beyond what they had asked for or expected to receive. As Dawahare said of Combs's and her own reaction, "we were both amazed, genuinely amazed at the sweeping and courageous decision."[55]

What are the implications of this conception of a right to education, with its focus on adequacy rather than equity? And does the Court's understanding of what constitutes an adequate education square with moral ideals about equal citizenship?

LEGAL RIGHTS AND MORAL IDEALS:
CONVERGENCE AND DIVERGENCE

The criteria for an adequate education that the Kentucky Supreme Court set forth are instructive for considering the relationship between the legal right to education that emerged in Kentucky and moral conceptions of that right. Building on the trial court decision and its select committee report, the state supreme court included in its decision a list of skills and capacities that an adequate education should instill in students.[56] This philosophically rich list focused on students' capacities rather than resources, which "broke new ground in education jurisprudence," and its level of detail set a particular course for education policy in Kentucky.[57] The seven capacities the court named could be interpreted to encompass a wide array of reforms; thus the decision did not dictate too much to the General Assembly, but the capacities were "specific enough to have muscle in them" to set parameters for the legislative remedy.[58]

The attributes of an adequate education that the court identified go far beyond the minimal skills, such as basic literacy and numeracy, that are typically named in school finance cases. The *Rose* decision adopted robust, aspirational, and broad-reaching goals for the skills students should acquire, including:

> sufficient oral and written communication skills to enable students to function in a complex and rapidly changing civilization; sufficient grounding in the arts to enable each student to appreciate his or her cultural and historical heritage; sufficient levels of academic or vocational skills to enable public school students to compete favorably with their counterparts in surrounding states, in academics or in the job market.[59]

These capacities span civic, cultural, and economic outcomes for education. But does the court's view of education entitlements support the right to education for equal citizenship that I have advanced?

One foundational point of convergence is the *Rose* decision's recognition of education as a positive right rather than a negative one. A negative right would have required only that the state not interfere with the provision of education by other parties. By treating education as a positive entitlement, the Kentucky Supreme Court held the state responsible for providing a particular type of education to students.[60] Whereas a negative conception of a right to education does not tell us nearly enough about who is responsible for providing students with a sound education, or about the scope of the opportunities they are entitled to have, the Kentucky Supreme Court was unequivocal on both fronts by making it clear that the state legislature is responsible for providing an adequate education to students, and by delineating what that education should entail.

The right to education for equal citizenship that I have advanced is more specifically addressed by the three capacities that have a civic orientation: communication skills necessary for students to function in a changing world; knowledge of economic, social, and political structures that they need to make informed choices; and knowledge of government processes that is required for them to understand issues affecting their local and broader community.[61]

The court's decision does not explicitly use the term *autonomy,* but its call for a curriculum that enables students to understand issues affecting their community and to make informed choices about them suggests a vision of citizens who make sound and independent choices about public policy. This coheres well with the idea of cognitive autonomy that I describe in chapter 2: individuals' ability to think critically, reflectively, and independently about collective decisions in the public sphere. The court also called attention to the relationship between education and citizenship by quoting key parts of the *Brown v. Board of Education* decision:

> "education is perhaps the most important function of state and local governments. . . . It is the very foundation of good citizenship." . . . These thoughts were as applicable in 1891 when Section 183 was adopted as they are today and the goals they express reflect the goals set out by the framers of our Kentucky Constitution.[62]

In these ways the court recognized the tight link between education and citizenship, and it followed Alexander's emphasis in the select committee report on the civic rationale for common schools: "The objective of unifying the people through education was recognized as a condition precedent to a strong and viable democracy."[63]

Yet the court's concern for civic education does not fully address the need for cognitive autonomy. It does not, for example, directly address the need for citizens in a just democracy to be intellectually flexible enough to revise their views in response to compelling new information and arguments from others. Furthermore, the civic-oriented capacities enumerated in the *Rose* decision do not address the ability to use public reason and to know when to depart from its norms in the face of significant background inequalities. Public reason helps to keep public discourse focused on accessible, reason-based claims that concern the common good. The court's statement that individuals should have sufficient knowledge to "function in a complex and rapidly changing environment" might be understood as an expression of concern for students' ability to coexist in a diverse society, which is a central rationale for employing public reason. But the capacities the court outlines do not address the need for reason-based, nonsectarian arguments as a matter of inclusiveness; nor do they signify when those norms should be relaxed so marginalized groups can make their voice heard.

The *Rose* decision also sets aside certain moral ideals about educational justice, most notably, more egalitarian conceptions of educational opportunity. By stipulating that students should have "an equal opportunity to have an adequate education," the court implicitly allows for inequalities above the adequacy threshold.[64] It expresses all seven of the capacities that constitute a right to education in sufficientarian terms ("sufficient knowledge to . . ."). As I discuss in chapter 2, this may not be troubling from a civic standpoint because citizenship skills are not highly positional and because the adequacy threshold can be set at a level high enough to enable citizens to participate in the public sphere on equal footing. Yet with respect to labor market outcomes, K–12 education is far more positional: having a merely sufficient education may not be enough to enable one to fare well in a competitive labor market. And this very concern about the positionality of education was a key argument for reform in Kentucky in the first place.

Kentucky's poor educational record, advocates argued, made it difficult for students to compete for jobs in neighboring states and left Kentucky at a crippling disadvantage in the competition for business investment and job growth. The court's decision clearly expresses concern for the economic returns to education: it prescribed "sufficient levels of academic or vocational skills to enable public school students to compete favorably with their counterparts in surrounding states, in academics or in the job market."[65] But the court's adequacy approach may be insufficient to realize this goal—especially in view of interstate and international academic achievement data that can influence job creation and economic growth.[66]

Rose's focus on adequacy rather than equity may cohere better with the ideal of equal citizenship than with equal opportunity in the labor market; even a decision that is celebrated as a crowning achievement of the school finance movement entailed some departure from what the best political morality may recommend. But the accomplishments and limitations of the decision are best evaluated in light of how the court-issued rights took shape in classrooms and communities.

MAKING *ROSE* RIGHTS REAL

Although the Kentucky Supreme Court's decision was a sweeping condemnation of the state's education system, it did not prescribe particular remedies. This deference to the legislature cohered with the Council for Better Education's strategy of focusing only on liability issues to avoid controversy over possible reforms.[67] Yet the legislature was not without outside guidance as it began to craft policy solutions. The General Assembly received specific proposals from the Prichard Committee via its report *The Path to a Larger Life: Creating Kentucky's Educational Future,* which made policy recommendations to address the issues that most concerned the state's citizens. This report had become part of the plaintiffs' evidence during the trial court hearing, and it shaped subsequent debates about remedies.[68]

To meet the court's mandate for an entirely restructured public education system, the governor and legislature formed a task force that led the policy reform process. The task force was divided into three committees, each led by an outside expert, to address the major facets of reform: curriculum, governance, and finance. These committees deliberately excluded interest groups and advocates to protect the process from partisan influence.[69] But the Prichard Committee continued to shape the process in informal ways, from advising on who might lead task force committees to bringing together a coalition of groups—including the teachers union, school board association, and PTA—to foster agreement among them. This "crafting behind the scenes" ensured interest groups' support of pending reforms and served as an important vehicle for public accountability, given the Prichard Committee's long-standing role as a trusted citizens advocacy group.[70]

The business community, lead by the CEOs of three major corporations in Kentucky (UPS, Humana, and Ashland Oil), also remained ardent supporters and watchdogs of the unfolding reform process. Carolyn Witt Jones, who was the executive director of the Partnership for Kentucky School Reform (now Partnership for Successful Schools), an education reform group founded by local executives in 1991, described their integral role in the reform process: "Companies stepped in and said, 'We're going to stand ready to make sure this legislation does continue" in the face of opposition to tax increases in order to have a more highly skilled labor force.[71]

The Kentucky Education Reform Act (KERA) was passed in April 1990 and took effect that July. In response to the court's declaration that the entire state school system was unconstitutional, the reform bill that emerged after this expedited legislative process covered all facets of public education, from property tax assessments to teaching credentialing to testing. I briefly summarize KERA's key parts, then focus on what these reforms have come to mean for students' right to an adequate education.[72]

The curriculum component of KERA entailed major reforms to the structure and content of instruction, including ungraded primary classes for first through third grade, writing portfolios, and new assessments via the Kentucky Instructional Results Information System (KIRIS), with rewards and sanctions for schools' performance. The curriculum committee most directly addressed the seven capacities the court had outlined as constitutive of an adequate education, treating them as the "backbone of everything we did."[73]

The parts of the reform that addressed governance were less connected to the seven capacities but did speak to key values expressed in the court's decision, especially regarding what an efficient education entails. One significant governance reform was that KERA prohibited school leaders from holding positions if they had immediate relatives working in the district, a controversial decision given the scope of nepotism in schools.[74] Other key governance reforms included provisions for school-site councils to give parents and teachers more control over staffing and curricular decisions, and an appointed state school commissioner to replace the previously elected state superintendent.

The finance component of KERA most directly grappled with the tension between equity and adequacy as distinct principles for distributing educational resources. The finance committee arrived at a three-level funding system known as "Support Educational Excellence in Kentucky," or SEEK. This funding plan aimed to ensure an adequate education for all students while enabling districts, within limits, to spend beyond that adequacy threshold by raising local tax revenue to reflect local preferences. The first level of the new funding scheme guaranteed each district a foundation grant, and it required local contributions through a minimum property tax rate, which the state would augment to compensate for any difference between the foundation amount and local revenue. The next level, called Tier I, then enabled districts to tax themselves to raise 15 percent more revenue than the foundation grant amount, with matching state funds to equalize districts' tax bases. The final level, called Tier II, allowed districts to raise revenues up to 30 percent above the Tier I amount via local taxes, but applied a cap limiting annual revenue increases to 4 percent.[75] The state's additional education spending, which increased by $1.3 billion in the first two years of KERA, was funded by state income tax changes and a sales tax increase.[76]

Additional revenue also came from a new mandate that required property to be taxed at its full market value; before KERA the state median property assessment rate was just 27 percent of current value.[77]

In keeping with the Council for Better Education's anti–Robin Hood stance, every district stood to benefit from this new influx of money. All districts were guaranteed at least an 8 percent funding increase in the first year of KERA and a 5 percent increase in its second year, which went a long way toward keeping class divisions at bay.[78] Because the state's largest districts were also its wealthiest, a more stringent equity stance might have resulted in funding decreases for almost 15 percent of the student population.[79] However, maintaining support from wealthier districts also meant tolerance for substantial inequality between districts, given that districts could raise as much as 30 percent in additional revenue on top of the foundation grant and Tier I funding.[80] Despite KERA's tolerance for potentially significant interdistrict funding inequalities, Kentucky has maintained a relatively small degree of intrastate inequality.

The sheer scope of KERA, and the speed and collaborative spirit with which it was passed, signaled a promising new era for education in Kentucky. As Michael Paris underscores, the legislators who drafted KERA acted with a sense that history was being made. The governor's comments after the announcement of the *Rose* decision demonstrate that feeling: "We have the opportunity to rebuild, to redefine education in Kentucky."[81] Many involved in the process described the moment as an unprecedented and lucky one of "the stars being aligned"; perhaps as a one-off chance to make sweeping, positive changes: "I'm not sure it will ever occur again in my lifetime. It was just, maybe spiritual, ethical. . . . Some star aligned that we didn't know was out there and got people thinking the right way for a change."[82] But how would the public receive these reforms, and what outcomes would follow?

IMPLEMENTATION CHALLENGES

As a result of the Prichard Committee's public engagement efforts, alongside business leaders' support for reform and extensive media coverage of school conditions, most Kentuckians rallied behind *Rose* before KERA was passed. But when it came time to implement particular policy measures, public support was understandably more tenuous. The various reforms that constituted KERA brought significant changes to classrooms, where teachers, parents, and students felt daily the impact of new policies. Primary school students found themselves in mixed-age classrooms, teachers struggled to prepare students for new tests before a matching curriculum was in place, and parents had new control over curriculum and staffing via school-site councils. Though many of the changes were certainly welcome—particularly increased funding for all districts, as well as half-day preschool for at-risk four-year-olds—other reforms were more controversial in practice, especially the state's new accountability system.

Advocates and public officials knew that maintaining public support for reform posed a public relations challenge: "We had to establish messages about what KERA really meant: . . . what it meant to be a kindergartner or four-year-old who was going to be in an early childhood education program, what the testing meant, why we were testing."[83] Other significant challenges followed from the new demands on teachers, including the difficulty of implementing a new curriculum, adjusting to the multi-age, ungraded primary school system, and incorporating portfolio assessments. As these different policies were being quickly implemented, teacher training programs, according to some observers, were not adapting their methods fast enough; nor did teachers have enough professional development opportunities to best implement the reforms.[84]

Over time some of the more controversial facets of KERA were repealed or phased out, including the ungraded primary system and portfolio assessments. But much of KERA has been retained in the more than two decades since its passage, in no small part due to the vigilance of advocates intent on holding elected officials accountable for realizing *Rose* rights. The Prichard Committee continues to play a significant role, as its associate director describes: "Our world changed significantly from advocates, rabble-rousers, complainers, to advocates for implementation."[85] The Council for Better Education, though less visible without the parent engagement programs that Prichard runs, also continues to serve as a watchdog and has gone back to court to challenge the legislature for not providing the adequate education to which Kentucky students are entitled. Moreland explained:

> You don't go to court too quickly, because people have to have an opportunity to work this system out. But I think in every politician's psyche, there's somewhere it says to them "If we don't try to make a good faith effort, those guys are going to drag us back to court, because they did the first time and they beat us good the first time."[86]

One of the most challenging parts of KERA to implement has been the funding goal of providing an adequate education for all students via the foundation grant and limiting, to some degree, inequalities among districts.

KERA provided a significant influx of money to schools throughout the state, but the multilevel funding system can achieve its adequacy goals only when it is fully funded. Some advocates worry that recent budget cuts have resulted in an inadequate foundation grant. This exacerbates inequalities between those districts that can raise additional funds through local taxes and those that cannot. "Adequacy is clouding the argument about equity because if the base is not strong enough, then everybody suffers," current Council for Better Education president Thomas Shelton said. "But, again, who suffers the most are the poorest districts."[87] Other advocates argue that a certain degree of equity—or, put another way, bounded inequality—has been easier to achieve than adequacy. According to Moreland,

> We've got reasonable equity, but we still haven't gotten any farther along with regard to adequacy, because we don't know exactly what we need to be adequately compared to. Do we want to be adequately compared to the seven surrounding states? Do we want to be adequately compared to all the money spent on education around the nation, or the world?[88]

These questions point to the philosophical complexity of the adequacy approach and to why it is essential to answer the question: Adequate for what? The *Rose* decision addressed adequacy for equal citizenship to some degree, but for political and legal reasons, the decision had to be less prescriptive and more general in outlining its conception of adequacy than theorists or policy makers might want. Even so, significant and concrete advances have come forth from *Rose* and KERA.

THE OUTCOME OF *ROSE* RIGHTS

It is not my purpose in this section to offer new empirical analysis of the outcomes of KERA or to engage in the ongoing debate about whether increased school funding yields achievement gains. Rather, I am chiefly concerned with how the rights claims that *Rose* advanced and that KERA institutionalized have shifted public thinking about education entitlements in Kentucky and influenced public engagement with education reform.

That said, brief mention is warranted for a few notable outcomes of KERA that indicate progress over the dismal condition of Kentucky schools pre-*Rose*. In 2009, Kentucky ranked sixteenth among U.S. states in per-pupil funding; it had ranked around 43rd before *Rose*.[89] Furthermore, the degree of intrastate inequality in Kentucky is small compared to that in other states.

According to recent analysis by Goodwin Liu, the spread between per-pupil spending in Kentucky districts in 2001–2 at the 10th and 90th percentile for such spending was only $1,000, compared to some $3,000 or more in Wyoming, New Jersey, New York, Connecticut, and Delaware.[90] Douglas Reed similarly found that funding inequality among Kentucky districts dropped by almost 45 percent between 1988 and 1995.[91]

Achievement gains on state standardized tests have been more difficult to measure since changes were made to Kentucky's accountability system, and state-level exams do not allow for interstate comparisons, given the variability in tests across states. Student scores on the National Assessment of Educational Progress (NAEP), a national test given yearly to a representative group of fourth- and eighth-grade students, are a more reliable indicator of achievement gains. In 2011, 72 percent of fourth graders and 79 percent of eighth graders in Kentucky scored at the basic level or higher on the reading portion of the exam, and their scores were above the national average.[92] That same year, 85 percent of fourth graders and 72 percent of eighth graders performed at the basic level or above in math; fourth graders' math scores were also above the national average, while eighth graders' math scores were one point below it.[93] These numbers mark significant progress from Kentucky students' low achievement prior to the reforms *Rose* prompted. In 1990, Kentucky was eighth from the bottom in NAEP performance[94], and it now falls in the middle of the pack in national achievement rankings.[95] In the eyes of reform advocates, this is just the beginning. The Prichard Committee's work is ongoing; it recently announced a new campaign that aims to move Kentucky's achievement into the top twenty nationally by 2020.[96]

Funding and achievement rankings can certainly be useful measures of progress in education reform, but less measureable outcomes of *Rose* should not be overlooked, especially in view of the value of educational rights from a democratic perspective. Two outcomes on this front stand out: increased public awareness of and engagement with education reform issues, and elevated public expectations for students' educational opportunities.

The *Rose* decision prompted a significant cultural shift in Kentucky with respect to public concern for and expectations of schools. The public mobilization surrounding *Rose* fundamentally altered many citizens' view of schools by prompting a transition from complacency about conditions to recognition of inadequacies, then to persistent calls for reform. And citizens' heightened concern for schooling conditions became a powerful force for accountability for public officials and led elected officials to take ownership of the sweeping reforms. As one of the architects of KERA, a former interim commissioner of education, put it:

KERA was such a major undertaking and there's so much ownership in it, particularly in the early years, that even though a new governor came in a year after it was enacted, that new governor did not try to undo anything about it. The next governor didn't. The next governor didn't. And then by the year 2000, KERA was institutionalized in the public schools.[97]

KERA fundamentally changed public education in Kentucky. But perhaps more important, it changed people's expectations for what schools can and should do—which keeps officials accountable for realizing and protecting students' rights to an adequate education. This shift in perspective grew out of the mobilizing efforts surrounding *Rose,* especially via the Prichard Committee, and also from the persistent support of the business community and the media's dedicated coverage of reform issues. From a democratic perspective, this web of support for *Rose* and KERA holds great promise for safeguarding rights over time and for generating new reform campaigns as needed.

Rose and KERA have faced and will continue to face significant political hurdles. The lack of a current lawsuit, coupled with the passing of time since KERA was enacted, may have dampened the public's vigilance over reform in recent years. As one observer noted, "The public is just much less interested in whether or not every single element of KERA is being implemented properly."[98] Kentucky's position in the middle of national achievement rankings may also work against public mobilization today: "Now it's us and Iowa, and what's wrong with that? It's a harder case to make."[99] In addition, the Prichard Committee now faces the challenge of finding a new role under new leadership twenty-plus years after *Rose* — a challenge further complicated during a time when people's primary concern may no longer be education, but rather the economy and the labor market.[100] Some advocates see the fact that the Kentucky Supreme Court, unlike the trial court, did not retain jurisdiction over *Rose* as a source of implementation challenges, and as the reason why the Council for Better Education tried (unsuccessfully) to initiate a new lawsuit in 2007: "We were desperately in need of going back to the well," explained Lavit, co-council on the original *Rose* case.[101]

On the other hand, some contend that the fact that *Rose* rights are institutionalized in the court's decision and in KERA has stopped politicians from cutting education funding during hard times: "You'd like to think politicians do that for magnanimous reasons," Moreland said, "but I think they all understand that . . . the Supreme Court has said that it's a fundamental right. If we go there, we're going to get sued tomorrow. So we'll cut everyplace else we have to cut."[102] Although the public's attention may be less focused on education reform now than it was two decades ago, KERA reforms are embedded in the public culture and in the legal precedent that *Rose* established. This ensures that students' right to an adequate education in Kentucky is unlikely to be violated without public uproar.

DEMOCRATIC CONCERNS AND JUDICIAL REVIEW OF RIGHTS

Community engagement, from the initiation of *Rose* through the implementation of KERA, has not only been central to the realization of students' educational entitlements, it has been important from a democratic standpoint, given long-standing concerns about the legitimacy of judicial review of education policy.

Reflecting on the *Rose* litigation, Alexander writes: "Possibly the most important conclusion that can be drawn from the Kentucky decision is that state legislatures in most circumstances are unlikely to provide equal educational opportunities without judicial intervention."[103] Before *Rose*, the state legislature had failed for decades to remedy the inadequacy of and inequality in Kentucky's education system. Many scholars agree that the systemic reforms in Kentucky were only possible, at least at that time, via judicial intervention. From this perspective, one can view the court as providing political cover for the legislature to act.

But there is an alternative to this celebratory interpretation of *Rose* that is concerned with the legitimacy of court-based reform and that questions whether it is democratically appropriate or effective for courts to circumvent the legislative process. A number of critics, speaking mainly from a conservative perspective, ground their opposition to court-based education reform in claims that judicial intervention has not raised student achievement.[104] These arguments rest on a contested empirical basis and are peripheral to the rights-democracy tension that frames my analysis. However, some criticisms of judicial review are internal to democratic theory and are thus especially salient to my arguments for a right to education.

Waldron's opposition to judicial review is a seminal perspective within liberal theory. Waldron is not opposed to the concept of rights; to the contrary, he is a leading rights theorist who gives pride of place to the right to participate in democratic decision making, which he calls "the right of rights."[105] His opposition to judicial review, then, stems not from an antirights stance but from democratic concerns.

Waldron's opposition rests on two grounds. His first objection is that judicial review is not democratically legitimate because it transfers authority from citizens to a select group of often unelected judges.[106] His second objection is that courts rarely engage in the careful moral reasoning that debates about rights deserve. Because courts are preoccupied with defending their legitimacy, he argues, their decisions focus on why they are authorized to decide the matter at hand and give short shrift to more substantive issues.[107] Waldron also worries that judicial review may prompt legislators to be cavalier about rights when they make policy because they may assume that courts will prevent rights-violating legislation from being implemented.[108] The legislative process, Waldron concludes, is therefore preferable to judicial review on two fronts: it doesn't suffer from a legitimacy problem, and it is more likely to "go directly to the heart of the matter" with substantive moral debates about the rights in question.[109]

Yet if we take seriously the notion of democratic participation as "the right of rights" and have a realistic appraisal of conditions in Kentucky before *Rose*, judicial review of educational rights in this instance was not only defensible but necessary. Waldron's concerns about judicial review can be readily overcome in this context for three reasons. First, the fact that education reform had been so long ignored in Kentucky, even though it was so badly needed, made a timely legislative response rooted in substantive moral debate highly improbable. As Waldron argues, rights theorists should be "uneasy about political arrangements that tend to silence" the voices of those whose interests are at stake.[110] There comes a point, which Kentucky had surely reached, when politics within a state legislature are more damaging to students' interests than is judicial review, especially given the disproportionate political influence of wealthier constituents and school districts.

Moreover, as litigator and legal scholar Michael Rebell has argued, concerns about the democratic legitimacy of court-based education reform in the United States are anachronistic today given the courts' longtime involvement in education cases and the public's acceptance of their role over time.[111] And in any case, the *Rose* plaintiffs did not go to court quickly. Guess approached superintendents to gauge interest in a lawsuit only after all other remedies had been exhausted, and Combs waited to file suit until it was clear that the legislature would not pass a reform bill.[112] As Lavit put it, "It had been in the political process for a hundred and some years. . . . They weren't going to do anything now."[113]

Second, questions about the democratic legitimacy of court intervention can be answered in the Kentucky context by the level of public engagement surrounding the litigation. The Prichard Committee held forums across the state for citizens to discuss their concerns about public schools and to make recommendations for reform. Public support for reform was hardly unanimous, but the content of the Prichard Committee's forums demonstrated a broad mandate for change that undercut concerns about the democratic credibility of the *Rose* plaintiffs. The Prichard Committee helped generate and sustain this mandate by prioritizing public engagement. "Running through all our recommendations is our firm commitment to the necessity of increased and deepened public involvement," it reported, including a call for indicators the public can use to evaluate schools, provisions for parental involvement in local goal setting, and support for using school buildings as community centers to facilitate partnerships with families.[114] Given the degree of public momentum surrounding *Rose* and the accountability pressures it created for elected officials, Waldron's worry that judicial review can lead legislators to be less careful about rights was not an issue: "Had it not been for citizens really getting up in arms about it, the results would have been different," one official said.[115]

Third, judicial intervention is warranted in this case because education entitlements follow closely from Waldron's concern for the right to participate in democratic governance. This point is central to the case I make in chapters 1 and 2 for why a right to education is a necessary precondition for a just deliberative democracy. Education is intimately connected to individuals' ability to participate in collective decision making as civic equals. To subject fundamental provisions for an adequate education to democratic deliberation, especially in the context of systemic background inequalities, would exacerbate those very inequalities by marginalizing some individuals in policy discussions about a social good that is integral to preparation for democratic participation. Given the centrality to democratic legitimacy of a right to education, then, judicial review is warranted when the legislature fails to recognize and safeguard this right.

This is the core idea behind John Hart Ely's seminal justification for judicial review of certain rights that are "representation reinforcing"—that is, integral to a fair democratic process.[116] As Joshua Cohen elaborates in the spirit of Ely's argument, judicial review may at times be the best way to protect individual rights; however, "it need not be seen as reflecting any hostility to democracy, or willingness to assign it an objectionably subordinate position, but might rather be seen as founded on a commitment to it."[117] This defense of judicial review mirrors my argument for a right to education: that it is essential to, rather than a constraint on, a just deliberative democracy.[118]

It is important to emphasize, as Cohen does, that a defense of judicial review that responds to Waldron's democratic concerns need not privilege court-based reform over the legislative process. On this point, Corey Brettschneider rightly argues that when judicial review is necessary to protect fundamental rights, it does entail a "loss to democracy," but this loss would be even greater if courts did not intervene.[119] From a democratic standpoint, it would have been better if the Kentucky legislature had been able to pass an education reform bill that served the interests of the state's least advantaged students without a court mandate. This outcome would have honored popular will more directly and could have allowed for more inclusive debates about the full range of reforms necessary to address citizens' concerns. From a policy perspective, a remedy that originated in the legislature also might have instilled in the public culture a greater ownership of reforms, perhaps reducing what some observers now see as public withdrawal from education issues in the absence of a pending legal case.[120]

When it is possible, then, reform through the legislative process is preferable to court intervention. But conditions in state legislatures are often not conducive to policy reforms that honor the rights of poor and minority students, given the disproportionate influence of wealthier constituents and districts. When the chance of legislative reform is as slim as it was in Kentucky, democratic objections to judicial review lose their force. Yet courts are not necessarily in a better position to protect students' rights, so my support for judicial intervention is context-dependent. Courts must have both the power and willingness to engage in debates about rights, but the conditions for effective judicial intervention may not be met in many contexts outside the United States. And within the United States, the prospects for successful litigation depend on legal precedent, the political environment, and the nature of the education clause in a state's constitution.

When courts can and do recognize educational rights that legislatures have neglected, their intervention should be celebrated as democracy-enhancing. Nonetheless, from a democratic perspective it would be better if legislators protected students' rights of their own accord—not only because of the "loss to democracy" that litigation entails, but because judicial intervention may stymie public engagement with education reform after a lawsuit concludes.

More populist forms of advocacy to realize rights have the potential to overcome the democratic difficulties inherent to judicial review, but they raise a different set of challenges. I next turn to a type of advocacy that works through regular democratic politics rather than courtrooms to advance students' right to education.

CHAPTER FIVE

Coleman Advocates for Children and Youth: A Case Study in Community Organizing

> We believe that all children have a right to have their basic needs met, to be educated and prepared for full participation in society, and that it is the responsibility of government to ensure that these rights are fully realized.
>
> —Coleman Advocates for Children and Youth

In the American imagination, the possibilities for instituting rights are often reduced to litigation because only legal rights are considered "real rights." Yet courts are not the only or necessarily the most effective venue for claiming and realizing rights in the education arena. Although it is celebrated as a model for school finance litigation, the *Rose* case illustrates the myriad challenges that the legal process entails, from the initial task of translating reform ideals into justiciable claims to ensuring that judicial remedies are implemented faithfully. The education community has been especially attuned to these challenges since the fiftieth anniversary of *Brown v. Board of Education*, which prompted celebration of progress achieved but also doubts about the effectiveness of court-ordered social reform. Skeptics rightly point to the institutional limits of courts as change agents, and to the ways in which deep and durable racism in the United States continues to frustrate equity-minded education reform.[1]

In recognition of these limits, scholars and advocates look to democratic activism that takes place outside of courtrooms and have increasingly focused on community organizing groups in recent years. Organizing groups engaged in education reform are proliferating across the United States, as is scholarship that examines their principles, strategies, and outcomes. Recent studies of such groups in urban centers like Los Angeles, Chicago, and Philadelphia emphasize how they can amplify the voices of marginalized parents and students who are otherwise ignored in education politics.[2] And by expanding the range of participants in education reform, these organizations may help revitalize participatory democracy at the local level while holding schools accountable for the needs of all students.

This chapter provides a case study of a highly effective community organization in San Francisco, Coleman Advocates for Children and Youth. Through analysis of Coleman's education reform campaigns I consider how such organizations help realize students' right to education, and how they leverage rights claims in their advocacy efforts. Unsurprisingly, rights claims are a ubiquitous rallying cry in community-based school reform movements in the United States. Advocates leverage the moral and political force of rights to assert the urgency of their cause, to mobilize others to take action, and to hold public officials accountable for school conditions. Yet research on community organizations and education reform has not given much attention to the role of rights claims, despite their prevalence in reform discourse.[3] Nor have political theorists sufficiently considered how such organizations can help realize deliberative ideals by advocating for rights, and how those ideals may need to be relaxed if advocates' calls for reform are to overcome the injustices they face. The purpose of this case study, then, is twofold: to demonstrate how rights claims can be powerful tools in democratic politics in the United States, and to suggest ways in which deliberative theory needs to be revised in light of the inequalities advocates face as they employ rights claims.

In the sections that follow, I explore the purposes and outcomes of educational rights claims expressed by advocates in the everyday settings of democratic politics—as they are asserted in city halls, invoked in community meetings, and chanted in the streets. Rights expressed in these contexts may seem merely aspirational compared to rights pursued in court. After all, such rights claims are usually more expansive than what would count as justiciable in court, and they often far outstrip current social provisions, too. But that is precisely the point in making them: to push us to see beyond current conditions and to envision educational opportunities as they should be.

Because of their political force and aspirational vision, rights claims have been influential in a number of U.S. social movements outside courtrooms, including movements for pay equity reform, same-sex marriage, and civil rights.[4] Although claiming a right hardly guarantees its realization, the act of claiming it has moral value, as philosopher Joel Feinberg emphasizes: "The activity of claiming . . . makes for self-respect and respect for others, gives a sense of the norms of personal dignity, and distinguishes this other-

wise morally flawed world from the even worse world of Nowheresville"—
a hypothetical place where no one has any rights.[5]

In my analysis of Coleman's education reform efforts, I consider how,
why, and to what effect it employs rights claims, and whether these claims
cohere with the norms of deliberative democracy. As I discuss in chapter 1,
political theorists often draw a sharp line between deliberative and nondeliberative forms of political engagement. Rights-based political activism
might seem to fall outside the scope of deliberative norms because of its
unyielding, individualistic, and impassioned character. As the work of Coleman Advocates for Children and Youth illustrates, however, the distinction between deliberative and nondeliberative forms of democratic activism is much more ragged in practice than theory suggests. Indeed, rights
claims are integral to bringing about the conditions that deliberative theory
requires, and rights-based activism sometimes succeeds where parallel judicial interventions are relatively limited. Recognizing the place of rights-
based activism within deliberative democracy in the United States is especially important now, given the expanding cadre of advocacy groups that
invoke educational rights, alongside growing calls for a more inclusive and
deliberative political process.

REVIVING LOCAL ACTIVISM:
AN INTRODUCTION TO COLEMAN ADVOCATES

Coleman Advocates for Children and Youth has been advocating for San
Francisco's youngest residents for over thirty years—a long time given the
short lifespan of most advocacy organizations.[6] Since the organization's
founding in 1975, Coleman's work has expanded from its initial focus on
juvenile justice reform to address a constellation of policy issues that affect
the lives of San Francisco's poor and minority children. These issues include
parks and recreation, access to child care and health care, and more recently,
affordable housing and public education. From 1978 to 2004, Coleman was
lead by Margaret Brodkin, whose politically savvy, often confrontational
style, and highly effective strategies earned the organization a national
reputation.

Although advocating for children might seem relatively easy in a pro-
gressive city such as San Francisco, demographics make it more difficult
than one might expect. Among major urban areas in the United States,
San Francisco has the smallest percent of children in its population, about
14 percent. And only about 19 percent of households in San Francisco
include children under the age of eighteen, compared to over 30 percent in

Los Angeles, Chicago, New York, and neighboring Oakland.[7] In a context where such a large majority of voters have little direct interest in children's services, focusing public attention and resources on children's needs presents significant challenges.

Over the years, Coleman has developed and sharpened a set of tools to meet these challenges. Most notable are its budget advocacy strategies. Because decisions about how to allocate public funds are the bottom line in politics, Coleman carefully scrutinizes and publicizes the content of San Francisco's city budget. It does this to hold public officials accountable for discrepancies between their professed priorities and their funding decisions, and to call attention to what it perceives to be wasteful spending that could be redirected to support children.

Budget advocacy of this nature is especially important because funding decisions are usually a zero-sum game. In one landmark campaign, Coleman was able to establish a dedicated source of public revenue for children's services. In 1991, the organization drafted a ballot initiative to pass the Children's Amendment in San Francisco, which sets aside 2.5 percent of assessed property tax revenue each year to be spent exclusively on services for children and youth. The initiative, which voters have reauthorized until 2015, made San Francisco the first city in the nation to guarantee annual funding for children's programs. The Children's Amendment funds an array of programs for children and youth, including after-school programs, arts programs, and early childhood education.

To bring about policy reform of this nature, Coleman has historically relied on the expertise of its staff to navigate local politics and to seize windows of political opportunity, but the organization also has a long-standing commitment to providing parents and youth with opportunities to exercise their own voices in the political process. Coleman's interest in empowering its constituents is partly strategic. Involving parents and youth directly in the structure of its organization shores up Coleman's legitimacy with its target communities and with public officials, who are less likely to view the organization as a group of out-of-touch policy wonks or top-down reformers. Coleman's ongoing efforts to engage parents and youth also demonstrate its commitment to a view of democracy that mirrors deliberative theory's emphasis on a widely inclusive public forum. This commitment is reflected in one of Coleman's guiding principles: that the "people most impacted by a problem must be the ones who determine and fight for the solutions."[8]

To involve citizens more directly in its advocacy campaigns, Coleman started a youth empowerment group in 1991, and a similar group for parents in 1994. The structure of these groups has changed over the years, but they consistently train citizens to become self-advocates by teaching them how to navigate local politics, frame and execute advocacy campaigns, and monitor city officials and institutions to compel greater public accountability. As Coleman has embraced more community organizing strategies in recent years, its parent and youth groups have gained more autonomy to select and carry out the reform campaigns that Coleman undertakes. Coleman staff continue to offer issue-specific training to parents and youth to guide the policy changes they seek.

By mobilizing parents and youth to be leaders within its organizational structure, Coleman provides citizens with skills and opportunities for direct engagement in local politics, where there is potential for more clear and immediate payoffs than with advocacy directed at the national level. This is especially true in the case of education issues, which so deeply affect families on a daily basis. Coleman's mobilization efforts also offer more meaningful opportunities for community involvement with the policy process than are usually possible in court-based reform.

The contrast between these two rights-based forms of advocacy is especially clear in San Francisco, where Coleman has initiated more expansive policy reforms than recent judicial intervention has been able to achieve in the same setting. *Williams v. State of California,* a state-wide class-action lawsuit over the inadequacies of school resources in California, was settled in 2004 after a four-year legal battle. The settlement defined what students' right to education minimally means in California in terms of basic resources: qualified teachers, access to current textbooks, and school facilities in decent condition.[9] It also created a community-based accountability system that enables any individual to report when these basic resources are missing from schools; this system augments inspections by public officials.[10]

This legal settlement and the rights it recognizes have improved students' opportunities in many California schools, but in San Francisco public engagement with monitoring these new rights has been minimal.[11] From the perspective of Coleman's education campaign director, Pecolia Manigo, this stems in part from the limited nature of the reforms the legal settlement advanced: "Nothing that we were fighting for had anything to do with *Williams.* . . . We didn't have anything really to draw on."[12] This stance may change as Coleman's campaign issues shift and other communities, including neighboring Oakland, have leveraged *Williams* rights more substantially.[13] But to date Coleman's strategies and reform goals do not align with *Williams* rights, and this mismatch has stymied community uptake of those rights in San Francisco given Coleman's prominence there.

Nonetheless, Coleman has successfully advocated for significant education policy reforms that address its constituents' concerns, including curricular changes aimed at students' readiness for college and careers. These achievements demonstrate the potential effectiveness of rights-based community organizing even when judicial interventions in the same context are more limited.

RIGHTS CLAIMS AT WORK IN LOCAL EDUCATION ADVOCACY

The truth of Ronald Dworkin's notion of rights as political trumps is clearly demonstrated in how Coleman frames its education reform campaigns. The trumping power of rights has two dimensions in the context of Coleman's work, which I refer to as the internal and external force of rights claims. Internally, rights claims raise individuals' awareness of the educational injustices they face and empower them to press for reform. Externally, rights claims can help advocates to gain the attention of public officials. However, in the broader context of electoral politics, morally charged rights discourse also carries liabilities that advocates must weigh when framing their campaigns.

RIGHTS AS INTERNALLY EMPOWERING: "WHEN YOU SAY IT'S A RIGHT, YOU FEEL STRONGER!"

Rights discourse helps Coleman to overcome a significant barrier to the engagement of parents and youth: their view that current conditions are inevitable or the most that they deserve. As Manigo emphasized, it is the norm rather than the exception for Coleman's constituents in San Francisco (African-American, Latino, and Pacific Islander families) to feel that the public education system is not serving them well. Yet because the school system is "very good" at making less advantaged parents feel personally responsible for the shortcomings of schools, "like it's your fault we didn't do our job," parents may be disinclined to press for change.[14] Rights discourse reminds parents that they are not necessarily blameworthy and that their children are entitled to better opportunities. As former Coleman executive director N'Tanya Lee described it, a central part of Coleman's mobilizing efforts entails helping parents and youth to recognize and then challenge what she calls the "bootstrap" framework, which assumes that students only need to work harder to secure better educational opportunities and outcomes.[15]

In this way, rights discourse in practice bears out an advantage of rights claims that philosophers highlight. By framing calls for reform in terms of entitlements rather than needs, rights discourse emboldens individuals so they are not mere supplicants. As Jeremy Waldron puts it, "the language of rights refers us to the full moral status of claimants in a way that the language of needs, taken on its own, does not."[16] By invoking rights claims, Coleman can inspire its constituents to feel the sense of entitlement that more advantaged parents regularly act upon, and thereby to overcome "the despair of reformers who can work much more effectively in an atmosphere of indignation."[17] Manigo often reminds parents that as taxpayers they should demand a better education for their children; this framing is far more empowering than need-based claims that convey dependency.[18]

When rights are invoked in advocacy campaigns, they also demonstrate the practical power of philosophers' view of rights as moral limits on "the harms and losses that any individual or group may reasonably be expected to put up with."[19] Rights draw a line around individuals' interests that should not be violated and thus serve as countermajoritarian checks. When Coleman presses a rights claim, it implicitly acknowledges the tension between rights and democratic rule and asserts the priority of a particular entitlement over popular will. For example, to claim that all children have a right "to be educated and prepared for full participation in society"[20] is to privilege that entitlement over countervailing forces. This designation of priority contributes to rights' empowering spirit because it emboldens rights claimants with the sense that "we all as human beings and all children deserve these rights just by virtue of being people."[21] Such claims demonstrate the force of rights as political trumps not only in external, political contexts, but also in terms of shaping individuals' sense of self as beings who are morally entitled to particular resources and opportunities.

Once parents and youth are mobilized to advocate for reform, rights claims give Coleman's constituents firm language with which to hold school staff and elected officials accountable for the changes they seek. Coleman has held workshops to inform constituents of their procedural rights in schools with respect to disciplinary policy, special services for students, and students' rights with police on campus. This training enables parents to remedy specific problems their children may face. Yet Coleman does not want its rights-based advocacy to be as individualistic as this approach, taken on its own, might be. So in addition to teaching parents about their right to advocate for their own children, Coleman strives to direct parents' attention to the root problems that call for system-wide reform. To facilitate this more expansive view of rights and reform, Coleman aims to recruit parents who look beyond the immediate needs of their own children to recognize the underlying injustices that affect other children too.[22]

Given the effectiveness of rights claims for empowering parents and youth, Coleman frequently invokes such claims when framing its work for and communicating with its constituents, whether at rights workshops, in its newsletters, or in its mission statement and guiding principles. For example, in 2009 Coleman successfully advocated the adoption of a district-wide policy that requires all high school students in San Francisco's public schools to take the courses necessary for them to be eligible to apply to state universities. In this campaign, Coleman insisted that all students have the "right to be prepared for college and a secure economic future."[23] Rights claims like this may not have courtroom standing, and Coleman's leaders recognize that this is a limitation with its external audience. Yet Coleman continues to leverage such claims because of their positive influence on parents and youth: "There has been a very strong trend among parent leaders. . . . Part of what gets them feeling strong is to say, 'You have a right!'"[24]

RIGHTS AS EXTERNALLY FORCEFUL: "WHEN YOU SAY IT'S A RIGHT, IT IS UNDENIABLE"

On the political stage—in public hearings at city hall, at school board meetings, and before local media—the moral heft of rights discourse can be especially useful for gaining the attention of San Francisco's voters and elected officials. As a former Coleman staff member put it, "We use that kind of phrase because it is stronger; it gets to the core. When you say, 'It's a right,' it is undeniable."[25] By insisting on the moral priority of the entitlements at stake, articulation of rights can help mitigate the power imbalance between Coleman's constituents and the public officials whose support they need. This is especially true in the education realm, where disputing students' entitlement to educational opportunities would be political death for public officials: "They just can't argue with it. What are they going to say, 'No, [students] don't have the right to it'?"[26]

Yet when Coleman's constituents voice rights claims to an external audience, they face several liabilities and challenges. First is the risk that strong assertions on behalf of particular groups of children or adults will meet fierce resistance. Children are a politically safe constituency for which to advocate, and politicians go to great lengths to be viewed as child-friendly. But this general support for children's rights can splinter if the subject of rights claims is modified in even seemingly small ways. As Lee noted, "There's a real difference between talking about the rights of children and the rights of families. When you leave the sphere of the rights of children, it sounds more militant; . . . when you start including the adults, . . . it's heard differently."[27] Moreover, even though the children in "children's rights" may commonly be understood to refer to the low-income and minority children who are Coleman's central concern, making this identification explicit can be a political nonstarter. Coleman and other child advocacy organizations, such as the Children's Defense Fund, have historically expressed their rights claims in race-neutral terms to avoid the criticism that rights "pit group against individual, one group against another, and group against state."[28]

But even the euphemistic framing of children's rights faces a long-standing criticism that can torment theorists and reformers who advocate welfare rights: that positive rights claims to particular resources are simply too expensive to realize. As Lee described it, "You're caught between a rock and a hard place, where you want to make these demands in the system and you know the resources aren't there."[29] This is especially difficult, she emphasized, because advocates' demands for education reform are often not significant relative to the dire conditions in some schools. When Coleman's youth group pursued a campaign for cleaner school bathrooms, for example, a host of other pressing problems emerged, including the need for more funds for violence prevention programs and computers in classrooms: "The competing demands were just ridiculous. . . . None of the things are superfluous."[30]

Aspirational rights claims that inspire parents and youth to democratic activism run the risk of being dismissed as utopian by Coleman's external audience, particularly in the case of "soft rights" whose violation is unlikely to be grounds for a lawsuit. Lee explained that advocates in San Francisco might look at the achievement gap between minority and white students, coupled with the declining minority population in the city, and be tempted to say, "We should just sue the city!"[31] But it is unclear whether legal rights have been violated in this instance. And in the absence of a firm legal claim, some voters and public officials may dismiss advocates' rights claims as toothless. Compared to the internal force of rights claims, their external force as they are voiced before a broader audience in San Francisco may be less powerful. Nonetheless, Coleman employs rights claims in both contexts because their unyielding nature can help reform goals gain traction in a political environment with myriad competing claims.

Yet it is precisely the rhetorical strength of rights claims that can bring them into tension with the ideals of deliberative democracy. Because I have located my arguments about educational rights in the context of a deliberative democracy, this potential dilemma warrants close attention. Advocacy organizations like Coleman show how deliberative theory may need to be revised in view of the obstacles that rights claims face on the ground. Attention to such revisions is especially important now, given the prevalence of rights claims in education reform efforts and growing interest in applying deliberative principles to the education policy process.

RIGHTS-BASED ACTIVISM AND DELIBERATIVE PRINCIPLES IN PRACTICE

If rights-based political activism like Coleman's does not completely comport with the principles of deliberative democracy, what does this mean for the possibility of advancing deliberative ideals, especially in education policy making? To answer this question, I return to the distinction between deliberative democracy and economic views of democracy—a distinction that political theorists draw sharply. Recall that the economic view assumes that citizens are irreversibly self-interested, so they promote their individual welfare through political bargaining. By contrast, deliberative theory assumes that citizens can follow the norms of public reason, focus on the common good, and be open to compromise when making public policy decisions. According to this view, the policy process is discursive, cooperative, and focused on the general welfare.

Deliberative Democrats and Democratic Activists

Iris Marion Young makes a related distinction between two views of democratic politics that is useful for analyzing the possibility of rights-based advocacy within a deliberative democracy. Young compares, at the level of practice, a deliberative democrat to what she calls a democratic activist. She portrays both citizens as deeply committed to social justice, a portrayal that reflects a more charitable view of citizens' motivations than economic theorists of democracy grant. In Young's account, the deliberative democrat participates in politics in a measured, reason-driven way, with an eye to the common good. By contrast, the democratic activist's strategies are more closely aligned with those of interest groups under the economic view of democracy, which pressure public officials to advance their goals.[32]

As Young depicts democratic activists, they are feisty, brazen, and focused on asserting the needs of the subset of the population with which they identify. Whereas deliberative democrats limit themselves to the power of the better argument to prompt reform, activists leverage whatever power they have (within reason) to advance their goals. The politically savvy activist has little faith in deliberation and "finds laughable the suggestion that he and his comrades should sit down with those whom he criticizes" to reason about differences and arrive at a consensus.[33] As activists see it, deliberation is not only ineffective; it also reinforces power hierarchies and thus exacerbates the disadvantages that marginalized citizens face.

The activist's criticism presents a dilemma for citizens who are committed to deliberative principles. Can reform-minded citizens engage in politics in ways that honor deliberative ideals, but that are not powerless in the face of systemic inequalities in educational and other opportunities? The starkness of the tension that Young draws between the deliberative democrat and the democratic activist suggests that this may not be possible. Although she acknowledges that she has exaggerated their differences for conceptual clarity, Young maintains that there is a fundamental difference between the two approaches to political engagement and, by extension, between the corresponding views of what good citizenship entails. Given these two seemingly distinct modes of democratic activism, how should we classify Coleman's claims about educational rights and its reform strategies, and what does this mean for the possibility of rights-based advocacy within a deliberative democracy?

Coleman's work suggests that in practice the difference between these two types of democratic politics may not be as great as theory suggests, especially in view of why and how Coleman leverages educational rights claims. The similarity between them is evident in the difficulty associated with classifying Coleman's work as clearly consistent with either the deliberative or the interest group model of politics.

First, consider how Coleman's educational rights claims might be at odds with core deliberative ideals. Coleman uses rights discourse to mobilize its constituents and to help them develop a critical analysis of disparities in educational opportunity, and it seeks to cultivate a group of parents and youth who, by acting on a strong sense of injustice, make ardent claims about the educational resources they deserve. In Lee's words, the organization should help "individual students yelling things like, 'I have the right to a quality education!'"[34] And in its recent education campaigns, Coleman has been more explicit about its focus on the needs of particular minority children and youth. In its advocacy for a mandatory college-preparation curriculum, for example, Coleman asserted that such a curriculum is a right of African-American, Latino, and Pacific Islander students, and that this curriculum must be implemented in such a way that it does not merely become "another systemic support for Asian, White, and other advantaged peers."[35]

One interpretation of these assertions is that they violate, or at least do not easily square with, the core principles of deliberative democracy because they advance uncompromising claims on behalf of particular groups and may even pit one subset of the population against another. As critics of rights see it, such claims limit rather than open up conversations among citizens, thereby undercutting the ideal of a widely inclusive and discursive political process. Mary Ann Glendon succinctly expresses this criticism: "For in its simple American form, the language of rights is the language of no compromise. The winner takes all and the loser has to get out of town. The conversation is over."[36] If we take Glendon's point seriously, rights claims are conversation stoppers that undermine deliberation.

Yet Coleman's work is also difficult to classify as entirely consistent with the interest group view of politics, which is the approach of the democratic activist. As Young depicts activists, they find the expectation of achieving reform through reasoned dialogue with those in power naive and futile. This does not square well with Coleman's advocacy efforts either, given the relationships it carefully cultivates with public officials. Even before former Mayor Gavin Newsom took office in San Francisco, for example, Coleman had worked carefully to focus his attention on children's issues through reasonable but firm arguments it presented in media outlets, newsletters, and public and private meetings. Before the election, Coleman held a forum for mayoral candidates in order to press them to focus on children's issues and was pleased to find that candidates were clamoring to hold a press conference about children's policy.[37] As Young portrays activists, they would likely view such activities as pointless, if not counterproductive.

The difficulty of characterizing Coleman's efforts as aligning with either the activist or the deliberative conception of politics reveals a gap between those conceptions. The interest group model of politics, as a subset of the economic view of democracy, is descriptive; that is, it is rooted in a view of how citizens actually operate—according to self-interest. By contrast, the deliberative model is aspirational in that it sets out a vision for how politics should function—through dialogue directed at the common good. Coleman falls between these conceptions: it is attentive to actual political conditions while it envisions a more just society emerging from those conditions. The interest group model fails to capture Coleman's faith in working with public officials and institutions to bring about meaningful change. Conversely, deliberative theory often fails to recognize that more contestation is needed to bring about the conditions that would make fair deliberations possible. To correct for this problem, we need not reject deliberation altogether but can instead relax deliberative norms to permit more contestation. This approach makes room for rights claims within a deliberative framework, and thus gives that framework traction in nonideal circumstances.

Advocating for Rights in the Face of Injustice

When background inequalities threaten the fairness of public deliberations, the norms for political engagement can and should be modified.[38] In such times, only "wishful thinking political fools" would adhere to deliberative principles that amount to "political disarmament," as Archon Fung puts it.[39] Yet when deliberative norms are being modified for imperfect conditions, a balance must be struck between political naïveté and political immorality. If deliberative theory is to be relevant in nonideal circumstances—which is to say, here and now—revisions are necessary that neither cast aside its ideals nor require adherence to politically naive reform strategies.[40]

Coleman's strategies for reform can be understood as striking this balance. In recognition of background inequalities that impede fair deliberations, Fung rightly advocates that the rules for deliberative activism should be increasingly relaxed in proportion to the magnitude of social injustice present, which is an argument he likens to the rationale for civil disobedience.[41] This perspective offers an interpretation of deliberative theory that condones certain types of contestatory protest activity that can bring about deliberative ideals, so long as the tactics used are proportionate to the obstacles impeding fair deliberations. Moreover, this view challenges the stark divide that theorists draw between interest group and deliberative politics by recognizing that nonideal circumstances may require activism that departs from deliberative norms, but that should not undermine them. This reframing allows us to amend rather than dispense with deliberative theory in imperfect conditions, and it makes room for rights-based education advocacy, like Coleman's, within a deliberative framework.

Coleman is committed to expanding the boundaries of who participates in local politics. The tactics it employs to achieve greater inclusion and public accountability, though sometimes bare-fisted, are far from anti-deliberative in that they never foreclose the future realization of deliberative ideals (as would, for example, strategies that include violence or libel). Furthermore, Coleman's reform goals convey an implicit faith in political institutions and officials because the organization depends on the targets of its advocacy to implement the policy changes it seeks. Making rights claims of the sort that Coleman presses, after all, implicitly suggests that someone has the capacity to realize those rights. Coleman's use of rights discourse thus resonates with Fung's concept of the "deliberative activist" who sees the need for advocacy strategies that are more forceful than reasoned argument, but still believes in the possibility of reforming public institutions and practice.[42]

It might be argued that Coleman could still be effective if it were to forgo rights discourse in favor of less muscular claims.[43] But given Coleman's constituency and its reform goals, there is little reason to dismiss its rights claims on the grounds that they undercut deliberative ideals. As I emphasize in chapter 1, structural inequalities in the United States, especially with respect to educational opportunity, prevent individuals from deliberating on equal footing. We only compound these inequalities if we exclude from reformers' arsenal strategies that are well-suited to bringing about more fair conditions for deliberation. As Young argues, theories of democracy should recognize the necessity of more aggressive contestation on behalf of marginalized groups: "We can conceive the exchange of ideas and processes of communication taking place in a vibrant democracy as far more rowdy, disorderly, and decentered."[44] This does not require a departure from deliberative ideals; indeed, it may help to create the conditions that deliberative democracy rests on.

Coleman's work shows how rights-based advocacy can advance deliberative ideals in U.S. politics, but it also raises a question: At the level of practice, can we distinguish between the activist who employs rights discourse in the spirit of deliberative ideals, and the activist who rejects deliberative ideals altogether? Coleman's use of rights discourse could be interpreted either way, but it fits well within a revision of deliberative theory that takes into account unjust conditions.

In the next and final section, I show that when Coleman engages with parents and youth around education reform, it employs rights-based advocacy strategies that are consistent with deliberative principles. These efforts demonstrate the sort of activities deliberative theory should make room for if we are to move closer to realizing its ideals.

CULTIVATING DELIBERATIVE ACTIVISTS

Lee explains that Coleman is trying to "create a model of social change that brings the best of . . . Democratic Party pragmatism with what some people might consider an old-school, self-determination of people of color, community control" model.[45] Coleman's recruiting efforts reflect its goal of drawing marginalized communities into politics rather than working with citizens who are relatively well-served by public institutions and policies. As a matter of principle, it does not seek out parent members from affluent neighborhoods in San Francisco because it does not believe that these parents should be dominating discussions about public education reform.[46]

Coleman thus has to contend with the thorny problem of how to get typically ignored citizens heard in the public forum, an issue central to some theorists' concerns about the legitimacy of public deliberation. This problem is heightened in Coleman's case because of its determination to influence public policy. Given this goal, Coleman staff must decide how much latitude to give to parents and youth in organizing efforts, and when to let staff direct campaigns to seize windows of political opportunity. Until recently, this decision was often made on the side of staff-led campaigns with fewer opportunities to engage parents and youth, as the Children's Amendment exemplifies. In that instance, Coleman had to collect enough signatures to certify its ballot proposition and then mobilize citizens to vote—hard work to be sure, but work that does not fundamentally challenge power dynamics in the policy process because it relies on the majoritarian electoral system. By contrast, Coleman's recent efforts put parents and youth at the helm and make for an approach to reform that is more inclusive than litigation. This raises new challenges in terms of how to engage parents and youth in ways that will lead to meaningful policy change.

How does Coleman meet these challenges, and to what extent do its strategies reflect and challenge deliberative norms? To promote its constituents' meaningful inclusion in local politics, Coleman could proceed in two ways. It could attempt to change the norms and venues for public discussions to incorporate marginalized citizens on their own terms. Or it could teach its constituents to couch their claims in language that appeals to elected officials on their terms. Coleman strategically does both in ways that serve deliberative ideals. In recognition of entrenched power hierarchies, Coleman offers parents and youth training that prepares them to navigate existing political dynamics as they advocate for school reform. But with the hope of changing the political process itself, Coleman also presses public institutions and officials for greater transparency, public accountability, and inclusion of community voices—goals that clearly resonate with the core of deliberative theory.

For example, when the San Francisco Unified School District began its search for a new superintendent in 2005, Coleman advocated for community participation in the selection process through a campaign it called "Our Schools, Our Superintendent."[47] Coleman offered both procedural and substantive reasons for including parents in the selection process. Consistent with Coleman's guiding belief that citizens have a "democratic right" to participate in decisions that affect their lives, it emphasized that parents are the "real stakeholders" in the school district and are entitled to contribute to decisions about public education.[48]

Coleman's director of parent organizing pointed to the shortcomings of the previous superintendent as one reason parental input was needed. At a meeting with parents, this staff member noted that the previous superintendent was a poor fit because she opposed reforms parents supported, like small schools, and did not understand San Francisco's rich ethnic diversity because she came from a city characterized by a black-white racial divide.[49] This mismatch, the Coleman staff member implied, could have been prevented had the school board consulted parents more thoroughly. Coleman's procedural and substantive rationale for a greater community voice mirrors Amy Gutmann's and Dennis Thompson's core concern for a democratic process that both is widely inclusive and yields outcomes that respect the interests of all citizens.[50]

To advance its goal of including more citizens in the policy process, Coleman confronts and addresses issues raised by critics of deliberative democracy. Young emphasizes that formal inclusion is unlikely to be enough to overcome the political disadvantages that some citizens face. Although the deliberative democrat might be comforted by sunshine laws and by public hearings in San Francisco that provide forums for deliberation, those mechanisms alone cannot ensure that the policy process is truly inclusive. Citizens interested in voicing their opinions obviously must know about such hearings, have the time and ability to attend them, and understand the conventions for participation.[51]

Coleman works carefully with parents and youth in advance of such meetings to empower them to offer evidence and arguments that are compelling to public officials. In addition, Coleman focuses on gathering a critical mass of citizens to attend meetings or to express their support by proxy in order to underscore the electoral stakes to public officials. For example, before Coleman parents appeared before the San Francisco school board to advocate their inclusion in the search for a new superintendent, Coleman collected over 1,200 postcards signed by San Francisco families in support of their cause. Coleman parents delivered these cards to the Board of Education along with oral arguments for why parents should be included in the selection process. Coleman staff did not risk having parents deliver extemporaneous comments; instead they culled concerns voiced by parents to draft a message that was read by parents at the meeting. The parents who testified said, "Our children are the actual stakeholders, the users of the sys-

tem, the clientele. We also have the most to risk. Most of us will still be de-
pendent on the public school system to educate our children long after you
have served your term in office. In other words, the schools belong to us."[52]

One might view this advocacy strategy as only dubiously deliberative
because some degree of paternalism is involved. As Coleman adopts more
community organizing strategies under its new leadership, it no longer
scripts parents' statements in this way.[53] Yet even if Coleman did continue
to do so, and if we take seriously the need to relax deliberative norms in
nonideal contexts, such preparation might be justified as a necessary step to
ensure that parents' arguments will resonate with politicians. It would be a
mistake to dismiss this approach as antideliberative given Coleman's goal
of broad inclusion in the policy process. Although Coleman has in the past
provided the script for parents' participation, it also has prompted public
officials to rethink how public hearings are structured to give parents more
voice. For example, Coleman successfully advocated that the school board
hold a series of public meetings in different parts of the city in order to
hear parents' views on the superintendent search. It pressed for this form
of public engagement because it worried that larger meetings at the school
district's central office might be an uncomfortable setting for parents to express their views.[54]

Coleman's way of engaging parents and youth in local politics seems
far more consistent with the qualities of a deliberative activist than with
those of a more typical activist, who would likely dismiss such meetings as
window-dressing. It might be argued that, given its long history and growing constituency, Coleman can afford to have faith in reform via public
officials and institutions. Newer organizations without Coleman's legitimacy would likely struggle more to capture officials' attention and to work
collaboratively with them toward reform goals. But this only underscores
the importance of making room for rights claims within deliberative theory
for nonideal circumstances, where power imbalances and background inequalities make it harder for some citizens to participate in public forums
on equal footing. Rights claims invoked in such contexts need not betray
deliberative ideals, but can help compensate for the conditions that would
otherwise undermine the realization of those ideals.

In this chapter I have emphasized how Coleman employs rights discourse outside the courtroom to advance a robust constellation of opportunities and resources for students. Taken together, they constitute what we
might envision as the education to which everyone has a right—an education that includes preparation for participatory citizenship, higher education, and employment. Coleman's accomplishments on this front are note-

worthy both for their substantive policy impact and for their influence on how the policy process is conducted. Now that I have considered rights claims pursued in two different venues, in the concluding chapter I highlight the need in the United States for collaborative rights-based activism that cuts across these settings to realize students' right to education.

CHAPTER SIX

Conclusion: Collaborating to Realize Rights

People mobilize around rights, not human capital policy. Every previous generation of reformers addressed its task in the language of citizenship and rights, as well as of budgets and policies. We have learned to be leery of high-sounding rights talk; we have not learned to do without it.
—William E. Forbath

Rights claims are politically and philosophically powerful tools for advancing social reform. They have been central to the most important social justice movements in the United States and are especially prevalent now in education reform discourse. However, the moral and political force of rights claims brings them into tension with a core principle of democratic governance: majority rule.

In the first part of this book I argue that the right to education should trump majority rule, and I describe what this right should encompass. I emphasize that because a robust right to education is necessary for equal citizenship, claiming it as a right should not be viewed as a constraint on democratic authority; rather, the right to education is a necessary precondition to a fair deliberative democracy.

I focus on the deliberative conception of democracy because of its academic and popular prevalence, and because it underscores the importance of taking seriously democracy's educational prerequisites; too often these prerequisites are ignored or understated in democratic theory, as are the realities of background inequalities that undermine fair deliberations. The aspirations in deliberative theory for a widely inclusive, egalitarian, and public-spirited policy process make significant demands of citizens and warrant treating the requisite education as a right, as it has been in historically important reform efforts.

The second part of this book has focused on realizing educational rights claims through the two most prevalent types of educational rights advocacy, which present a variety of opportunities and challenges. Advocating for educational rights in court carries the advantage of the imprimatur of the law, which in Kentucky was critically important for achieving reform through the legislative process. Winning judicial recognition of a right also gives claimants a clear path for recourse when that right is violated. Yet court-based education reform is vulnerable to a number of theoretical and practical criticisms. Although concerns about the democratic legitimacy of judicial review are often overblown in the education arena given the scope of inequalities and inadequacies that persist today, court-based reform is typically less inclusive than its alternatives because litigation is managed by legal professionals. However, judges and lawyers cannot single-handedly bring judicial remedies to fruition. As the *Rose* case illustrates, successful litigation for and implementation of educational rights depends on community engagement.[1] This engagement may not be forthcoming if the rights claims that positive law supports do not address core community concerns about educational opportunity.

By contrast, rights claims that community organizers advance in the everyday settings of democratic politics—in the streets, in community meetings, at city hall—can be more expansive, whatever positive law might say. San Francisco's Coleman Advocates for Children and Youth aims to empower parents and youth to be self-advocates, so its reform efforts often have a more populist character than typical litigation efforts. Coleman's rights-based reform campaigns are thus less vulnerable to concerns about democratic credentials. But the success of these efforts depends upon the whims of electoral politics. Coleman must win the support of public officials and voters to institutionalize its reform goals. And because Coleman asserts rights claims that do not have the force of law behind them, those claims may not gain traction in a political arena filled with competing interests. As a result, advocates' aspirational rights claims may be morally empowering for their claimants but turn out to be politically toothless.

In many ways the strengths and weaknesses of court-based reform and community organizing mirror each other. Neither type of advocacy is likely to realize single-handedly students' right to a high-quality education.[2] So why don't litigators and community organizers work together more to realize the educational rights they aim to achieve? On this front, Kentucky stands out, given the collaboration and overlap between the Council for Better Education's legal advocacy and the Prichard Committee for Academic Excellence's public engagement efforts. In many other contexts, however, as implementation of the *Williams* settlement in San Francisco demonstrates, these two types of rights-based reform strategies do not readily intersect in mutually reinforcing ways. I conclude by identifying some of the challenges and opportunities such collaborations present.

CHALLENGES TO JOINT ADVOCACY EFFORTS

A foundational obstacle to partnerships between community organizers and litigators stems from their different views of rights. Lawyers are trained to think of rights in terms of their justiciability, meaning in terms of what entitlements are likely to have legal standing in court. The necessity of translating educational injustices into legally viable claims can be a significant constraint on the scope of rights that can be pursued through litigation. Legal translation compels advocates to make pragmatic distinctions between ideal and realistic goals and supports the pursuit of attainable rather than aspirational rights.[3]

Litigators for the Council for Better Education were keenly aware of how their claims should be tempered given the difficulties that equity lawsuits in other states had recently faced and the potential for allegations that the court had overstepped its boundaries if it heard particular remedies advocated by reformers. As attorney Debra Dawahare described it, "We wanted to be careful in this lawsuit that we didn't in any way suggest that it was the province of the courts to form or to develop the details of the economic agendas for the public schools."[4]

Community organizers may adopt a more aspirational view of rights. This is evident in Coleman's reform campaigns—for example, when it claimed that all students have a right to be prepared for college—and is also a feature of national reform efforts such as Robert Moses's Algebra Project, which centers on the notion that math literacy is a civil right. Such advocacy groups are not only free from the limits of what positive law can support; they may choose to downplay or ignore positive law if they view its limits as emblematic of the political system they are pushing against. In this spirit, Coleman's former executive director N'Tanya Lee noted the advantage of invoking human rights instead of constitutional rights in their reform efforts because Coleman does not want to convey to parents and youth that their entitlements are bound by existing laws. The message they want to send is: "You do have the right. It's just not real yet."[5]

These divergent conceptions of rights stem from the different professional norms of community organizers and litigators and can frustrate collaborations between them. For example, although litigation begins with complaints about injustices that arise from individuals' everyday experiences, the hierarchical structure of the legal profession and the skills required to have a leading role within it limit the ways in which parents and youth can participate in court-based education reform. The Prichard Committee provides a model for how public engagement can occur alongside and reinforce litigation, but even in the case of *Rose*, citizens' participation in the legal process was limited due to the intricacies of framing and arguing legal claims. Jack Moreland, president of the Council for Better Education during *Rose*, said, "I don't think the rank-and-file person . . . knew and understood the legal side of it."[6]

This distance between legal efforts and public engagement stands in contrast with the goals of an organization like Coleman, which strives to empower its constituents to frame and execute reform campaigns on their own terms. Coleman remains interested in achieving policy change that institutionalizes its reform goals, but this interest increasingly comes second to its concern for preparing parents and youth to be self-advocates. Privileging process over outcomes, or at least giving them equal consideration, is not the orientation of most lawyers, who understandably focus on achieving a courtroom victory.

This contrast between litigation and organizing yields different points of entry for parents and youth who want to effect educational change. Many community groups, especially at the grassroots level, seek community input at all stages of the advocacy process and regard their work as inauthentic if it seems "top down." This orientation means that parents and youth are involved with, if not leading, reform efforts from start to finish. By contrast, litigators may have a more instrumental view of community involvement. They may recognize its importance when framing legal complaints and implementing judicial remedies, but the formal legal process provides fewer opportunities for ongoing public engagement.

These differences can create the tension between litigators and community groups that scholars have documented across a range of social movements.[7] To the community activist, litigation may seem at best to be an ineffective lever for social change, and at worst a counterproductive strategy that detracts from more promising alternatives. From this perspective, litigation comes up short because it reduces social injustices to unfamiliar legal terms, cedes control of reform to professionals, and yields solutions that courts cannot readily enforce.

Moreover, activists may believe that litigators use marginalized citizens just to have names, faces, and stories to attach to their legal claims. In doing so, litigators may crowd out more meaningful public engagement and may deradicalize social movements by pursuing less visionary goals.[8] John Lewis, a leader of the Student Nonviolent Coordinating Committee and now a member of the U.S. Congress from Georgia, poignantly underscored how some activists felt about this tension during the civil rights movement:

> This nation is still a place of cheap political leaders who build their careers on immoral compromise and ally themselves with open forms of political, economic, and social exploitation. . . . Mr. Kennedy is trying to take the revolution out of the streets and put it in the courts.[9]

Coleman staff did not express nearly this degree of frustration with court-based education reform. But they did convey that their reform strategies do not readily square with filing lawsuits, which is evident in their limited engagement with the *Williams* case in San Francisco. And the Prichard Committee did not immediately join forces with the Council for Better Education given its different approach to and initial skepticism about achieving reform via litigation. Cindy Heine, associate director of the Prichard Committee, recalled the reservations of both the Committee's namesake founder and its first executive director: "They didn't see litigation as the answer to getting where we needed to go."[10]

On the other hand, litigators involved in "cause lawyering" may be more likely to embrace partnerships with community organizers and to recognize their value than vice versa. As Dawahare put it, "if you want to do one of these lawsuits you do need to take the temperature out there, and then you need to do the kind of groundwork that the Prichard Committee and those town forum meetings did. . . . Otherwise I think you are in political peril from the beginning."[11] Even so, partnerships between litigators and community groups can be difficult to forge not only because of organizers' reservations, but also because of how litigators may perceive them and their strategies—especially when it comes to groups working with youth.

From a lawyer's perspective, one obstacle is that organizations like Coleman may change campaign issues frequently in response to students' interests. To a litigator accustomed to lengthy legal processes, this timeline can seem too short for achieving significant reform. Moreover, litigators may view community organizers' goals and tactics as too radical to gain political legitimacy. And organizers' focus on empowering individuals may seem to be an inefficient and unfocused reform strategy that does not yield broader change, especially when their campaigns are focused on narrowly local rather than city- or state-wide issues. In sum, from a litigator's perspective, community groups that take their cues from constituents' concerns can seem fleeting or episodic and lacking in the political traction and continuity of mission that seem necessary to bring about policy change.

The litigators involved with *Rose* did not express reservations about organizing nearly as strongly as I have presented them here, arguably in part because of the political legitimacy and influence of the Prichard Committee. Nonetheless the Council for Better Education and the Prichard Committee, though united by a common cause, pursued distinct paths to achieve school reform. Divergence between litigators and organizers is even more pronounced in the context of San Francisco, where Coleman's involvement with the *Williams* litigation was limited and no other community group has led a campaign focused on enforcing the rights that came forth from the *Williams* settlement.[12]

OPPORTUNITIES FOR COLLABORATION

The tensions I have described can be significant obstacles to collaborations between lawyers and community groups, but they are not insurmountable, and are often overstated. Litigators and community organizers share some common ground that can facilitate meaningful partnerships to advance education reform, as the events surrounding *Rose* illustrate. My purpose in highlighting these commonalities is not to support an overly rosy appraisal of the path ahead, but to point out how these types of advocacy can be mutually reinforcing if we adopt a more expansive view of educational rights and of who can advocate for them and in what venues.

The difference between the rights that have legal standing and the rights that community organizers may advocate narrows once we recognize that both types of rights are rooted in moral claims about what citizens are owed in a just democracy. As I emphasize in chapter 4, legal mobilization is unlikely to emerge directly from a sense that one's legal rights have been violated. Rather, legal mobilization is typically motivated by individuals' moral outrage—the sense that one has not been treated fairly. Moral claims about educational injustice, then, are the foundation for both legal advocacy and organizing efforts. Recognizing this common ground challenges the view of litigators as moderate reformers whose agenda is beholden to positive law. A realistic view of the constraints facing community organizers further narrows the distance between the rights claims pursued through organizing and litigation. Just as lawyers must translate their reform ideals into justiciable claims, so too must organizers frame their goals in terms that will be compelling to elected officials and voters. Both types of advocates mobilize citizens with moral claims about students' entitlements, and then must filter those claims in view of the constraints they face.

Recognition of these constraints points up another commonality between litigators and organizers in the education arena: they both can win recognition of new rights by pushing the boundaries of existing entitlements. This is worth emphasizing in view of the criticism that litigators are too constrained by positive law to bring about new rights, or conversely that organizers' rights claims are too idealistic to yield policy reform. Both types of advocates navigate challenges in order to extract new or expanded entitlements from recognized rights. The Kentucky Constitution holds the state responsible for providing an "efficient" education; from this, *Rose* litigators were able to define and institutionalize what constitutes an adequate education in Kentucky in terms of preparation for citizenship, the labor market, and further educational opportunities. Community organizations like Coleman similarly may establish new rights through political channels, as Coleman did when it won passage of a district-wide policy that requires all San Francisco students to follow a college preparatory curriculum. Neither litigators nor organizers are unconstrained in their pursuit of rights, but neither are too constrained to expand existing entitlements in ways that yield meaningful changes to law and policy.

A related and significant point of convergence between litigators and organizers follows from their role in implementing newly won rights. A classic criticism of "cause lawyering" and organizations like the ACLU is that they litigate and then leave, giving little attention to whether legal remedies make a difference on the ground. This criticism is outdated now in the decades since *Rose*, as litigators increasingly recognize the importance of seeing judicial remedies through to implementation. But remaining involved through implementation presents new challenges for litigators as they take on roles that organizers usually perform, such as providing political education about rights and mobilizing individuals to leverage them. Research on how lawyers can perform these roles in the context of social movements has grown over the last several decades.[13] The challenges are significant, especially the task of earning the trust of community members who view lawyers as outsiders or even adversaries. Community organizers may also face problems earning the trust of community members and mobilizing individuals to leverage their rights. These shared challenges have the potential to bring together litigators and organizers in ways that could enhance the effectiveness of both types of advocacy.

Organizers no less than litigators must balance concern for policy implementation with the need to conserve time and resources for new initiatives. And as lawyers increasingly recognize the importance of staying engaged through the implementation process, so too do community groups grapple with the challenge of ensuring that their hard-won policy victories make a difference months and years later.[14] As Coleman's education campaign director Pecolia Manigo said, "it's not enough to just get the policy passed," so the organization is lengthening the horizon of its education reform campaigns to multiyear efforts.[15]

Similarly, the Council for Better Education continues to monitor the conditions of public education in Kentucky and will return to court if education "is becoming a second-class citizen" and "we feel like we have to in order to make sure that we adhere to the fundamental success we've had through the supreme court ruling," Moreland said.[16] Litigators and community organizers taking a longer view of reform and implementation is a critically important step toward making hard-won educational rights more meaningful in classrooms. And this growing commitment to implementation on the part of both types of advocates bodes well for future partnerships between them if implementation challenges continue to necessitate joint efforts to advance educational justice.

This is especially true with respect to the many school finance lawsuits across the country. In this arena, reformers are increasingly calling for collaborations between litigators and community groups to ensure that judicial remedies are more than "paper rights." As a report recently issued by the Public Education Network notes, lawyers may win in courtrooms but community groups "must win in the court of public opinion."[17] This report also cautions that partnerships are needed from the very start of the legal process if the rights that are pursued in court are to become meaningful in communities. The Prichard Committee's public engagement work that predated and later intersected with the Council for Better Education's litigation is one model; another is the lawsuit brought forth by the Campaign for Fiscal Equity in New York (CFE). As its case in New York was unfolding, CFE held public forums throughout the state to solicit input from citizens about the needs of their schools and about what a "sound basic education" under the state constitution should encompass. This multiyear public engagement process shaped the claims that litigators pursued and continues to keep pressure on the legislature and courts for fiscal reform.[18]

IMPLICATIONS FOR DEMOCRACY,
EDUCATIONAL RIGHTS, AND CITIZENSHIP

Advocacy efforts that bring together legal and organizing strategies have the potential to mitigate the tension I have highlighted throughout this book between rights claims and democratic governance. This tension arises because rights claims constrain what democratic bodies may decide. Concerns about judicial review are the most prevalent expression of this tension in American politics today: critics argue that courts that overturn laws and public policy undermine the democratic process and flout popular will. Such concerns continue to mount in the education arena in response to school finance lawsuits.[19] In defending court-based education reform as a second-best solution, I acknowledge that this strategy for realizing students' rights would be unnecessary in more ideal circumstances. But we are far from this ideal today, so judicial review has an important role to play, and it can be made more or less democratic depending on the scope of community engagement surrounding court-based reform.

When the popular mobilization that organizing entails motivates and shapes legal claims, then many of the classic concerns about judicial review can be undercut—both from the perspective of those who question welfare rights generally and from the perspective of skeptical organizers who see litigation as a reform process led by elites. Community organizing also has important democratic value because it can advance a vision of participatory citizenship.

The process of recognizing and claiming rights can be a deeply empowering experience for individuals who are marginalized in education politics. It can also be a collective and community-enhancing process despite critics' claims about the atomistic nature of rights claims.[20] This is especially true of community organizing efforts in the education arena, which at their best bring together diverse groups of citizens, allow them to voice their shared concerns, and advance reform that addresses those concerns, as was the case in Kentucky. And the process of participating in rights-based advocacy is educative itself because it enables participants to learn about their rights and how to bring them to fruition. Participatory rights-based advocacy, then, advances the very ideal of deliberative citizenship that the right to education I have endorsed is tailored to cultivate. Third-sector organizations like Coleman, the Prichard Committee, and the Council for Better Education have an important role as civic educators, and the robust educational rights they advocate can bring back to the fore the civic purposes of public education at a time when those purposes are being eclipsed by concern for individuals' position in the labor market and the U.S. position in a global economy.

Yet even if the right mix of advocacy strategies is employed, and even if democratic concerns about rights-based reform can be addressed by the bringing together of litigation and organizing, a moral dilemma remains. Both of these forms of democratic activism target government at the city or state level. But my arguments for a right to education for equal citizenship necessarily apply across city and state boundaries because citizenship is a national matter.[21] Advocacy at the local level has its advantages, politically and legally. But work at the local level, if it does not spread up and out, places a premium on the community into which children are born and educated, which is arbitrary from a moral perspective. To be sure, students in Kentucky are better off today post-*Rose* than they might otherwise be. But what about students in Mississippi, which remains at the bottom of educational rankings by most metrics? It is important to think about how local efforts might be scaled up to break the links between educational opportunity and geographic happenstance. The right to an education for equal citizenship applies to children wherever they are educated—in Manhattan, Michigan, or Mississippi.

In the United States, the central obstacle to realizing educational rights that are not constrained by a child's residence is a historic and carefully guarded commitment to local control, which is the third rail in American educational politics. This commitment is frequently invoked by politicians in some form of the statement that local communities know better than the federal government. And it has the imprimatur of the U.S. Supreme Court, which declared in the *Rodriguez* decision: "Local control means . . . the freedom to devote more money to the education of one's children. Equally important, however, is the opportunity it offers for participation in the decision-making process that determines how those local tax dollars will be spent."[22]

As the movement for school finance reform has made abundantly clear, local control—especially and most significantly as it pertains to funding via local property taxes—yields a public school system with vast inequalities within and, increasingly, between states. And these inequalities extend not only to funding, but also to the academic standards to which students are held.[23] And as a decade of No Child Left Behind has demonstrated, what counts as proficient achievement differs vastly between Mississippi and Massachusetts.

Recent shifts in federal policy suggest that change on this front may be more likely now. Setting aside the substantive merits and problems of No

Child Left Behind and, more recently, Race to the Top, these policies mark a distinct movement toward greater federal control of education policy. And the Common Core State Standards, which have been adopted by forty-five states and Washington, DC, are well positioned to address the unevenness among state-level curricular standards.[24] To be sure, concerns about equal citizenship are rarely front-and-center in political rhetoric surrounding such polices because anxieties about global competiveness tend to dominate.[25] Nonetheless, national curricular standards, coupled with growing acceptance of, or at least acclimation to, greater federal involvement in education may weaken public commitment to local control and open new possibilities for realizing the ideal of educational opportunity for equal citizenship as a collective national concern.[26]

It is unclear whether further progress will come from the judiciary (for example, if the Supreme Court is willing to revisit *Rodriguez*); whether a legislative remedy is possible in the form of an amendment to the federal constitution; or if mounting concerns about educational inequalities and inadequacies might coalesce into an influential social movement with traction at the national level. Whatever the next steps might be, scholars and reformers must recognize and grapple with the complicated relationship between educational entitlements and political equality. The educational demands of democratic citizenship are age-old concerns that warrant renewed attention in thought and in action. Rights give us a moral vocabulary with which to express our aspirations for education for democratic citizenship and, by extension, for a more just society. They also empower individuals to lay claim to the education they deserve here and now.

NOTES

INTRODUCTION

1. Ronald Dworkin, *Taking Rights Seriously* (Cambridge, MA: Harvard University Press, 1977), xi.

2. Interview with N'Tanya Lee, former executive director of Coleman Advocates for Children and Youth, January 31, 2007.

3. San Antonio Independent School District v. Rodriguez, 411 U.S. 1 (1973), which I discuss in chapter 3.

4. Bruce Ackerman, *We the People: Foundations* (Cambridge, MA: Belknap, 1991), 12.

5. For example, see Philippe Van Parijs, "Why Surfers Should Be Fed: The Liberal Case for an Unconditional Basic Income," *Philosophy and Public Affairs* 20, no. 2 (1991): 101–31; Norman Daniels, *Just Health Care* (Cambridge: Cambridge University Press, 1985); Jeremy Waldron, *Liberal Rights: Collected Papers, 1981–1991* (Cambridge: Cambridge University Press, 1993), 309–38.

6. See Eamonn Callan, *Creating Citizens: Political Education and Liberal Democracy* (Oxford: Oxford University Press, 1997); Meira Levinson, *The Demands of Liberal Education* (Oxford: Oxford University Press, 1999); Rob Reich, *Bridging Liberalism and Multiculturalism in American Education* (Chicago: University of Chicago Press, 2002).

7. For example, see Jeannie Oakes and John Rogers (with Martin Lipton), *Learning Power: Organizing for Education and Justice* (New York: Teachers College Press, 2006); Mark R. Warren and Karen L. Mapp, *A Match on Dry Grass: Community Organizing as a Catalyst for School Reform* (New York: Oxford University Press, 2011); Mark Warren, *Dry Bones Rattling: Community Building to Revitalize American Democracy* (Princeton, NJ: Princeton University Press, 2001); Kavitha Mediratta, Seema Shah, and Sara McAlister, *Community Organizing for Stronger Schools: Strategies and Successes* (Cambridge, MA: Harvard Education Press, 2009); and Dennis Shirley, *Community Organizing for Urban School Reform* (Austin: University of Texas Press, 1997).

8. Such efforts include a major conference hosted by University of California–Berkeley School of Law, which brought together leading scholars and civil rights attorneys to discuss the contours of a right to education in 2006; reports by the Public Educa-

tion Network on public engagement with school finance litigation; and renewed attempts by organizations like the Southern Education Foundation to press for a constitutional amendment that recognizes a federal right to education.

9. Interview with Sandra Fewer, former staff member of Coleman Advocates for Children and Youth, December 19, 2006.

CHAPTER ONE

1. For recent work on this tension, see Corey Brettschneider, *Democratic Rights: The Substance of Self-Government* (Princeton, NJ: Princeton University Press, 2007); Thomas Christiano, *The Constitution of Equality: Democratic Authority and Its Limits* (Oxford: Oxford University Press, 2008); and David Estlund, *Democratic Authority: A Philosophical Framework* (Princeton, NJ: Princeton University Press, 2008).

2. My arguments in this chapter build upon ideas I developed in "All Together Now? Some Egalitarian Concerns about Deliberation and Education Policy-Making," *Theory and Research in Education* 7, no.1 (2009): 65–87; and in "A Democratic Framework for Educational Rights," *Educational Theory* 62, no. 1 (2012): 7–23.

3. For example, see Archon Fung, *Empowered Participation: Reinventing Urban Democracy* (Princeton, NJ: Princeton University Press, 2004); Shawn W. Rosenberg, "Types of Discourse and the Democracy of Deliberation," in *Deliberation, Participation and Democracy: Can the People Govern?* ed. Shawn W. Rosenberg (New York: Palgrave Macmillan, 2007); Lorraine M. McDonnell and M. Stephen Weatherford, "Seeking a New Politics of Education," in *Rediscovering the Democratic Purposes of Education*, ed. Lorraine M. McDonnell, P. Michael Timpane, and Roger Benjamin (Lawrence: University Press of Kansas, 2000).

4. For a collection of statements about deliberative democracy, see James Bohman and William Rehg, eds., *Deliberative Democracy: Essays on Reason and Politics* (Cambridge, MA: MIT Press, 2002).

5. Thomas Christiano uses this term to describe conceptions of citizenship and democracy that assume that citizens are self-interested. I draw upon Christiano's survey of these views here; see Christiano *The Rule of the Many: Fundamental Issues in Democratic Theory* (Boulder, CO: Westview, 1996), 131–59.

6. Joseph Schumpeter, *Capitalism, Socialism, and Democracy* (New York: Harper and Brothers, 1947), 253.

7. Amy Gutmann, "Deliberative Democracy and Majority Rule: Reply to Waldron," in *Deliberative Democracy and Human Rights*, ed. Harold Hongju Koh and Ronald C. Slye (New Haven, CT: Yale University Press, 1999), 232.

8. Many conceptions of deliberative theory do not dispense with voting altogether. Nonetheless, since voting is secondary in importance to public deliberation, citizens (the theory hopes) will reflect on and revise their views through public discourse, and will be faithful to the best arguments and to the common good at the polls.

9. For analysis of the conflict between individual and collective educational goals in the United States, see David Labaree, "Public Goods, Private Goods: The American Struggle over Educational Goals," *American Educational Research Journal* 34, no. 1 (1997): 39–81.

10. For John Rawls's much-debated idea of public reason, see Rawls, *Political Liberalism* (New York: Columbia University Press, 1996). For Gutmann and Dennis Thompson's application of this conception (in their terms, "reciprocity") to their view of deliberative democracy, see Gutmann and Thompson, *Democracy and Disagreement* (Cambridge, MA: Belknap, 1996), 52–94.

11. For example, Iris Marion Young and Lynn Sanders emphasize how public reason privileges white males at the expense of women and minorities; see Young, *Inclusion and Democracy* (New York: Oxford University Press, 2000); and Sanders, "Against Deliberation," *Political Theory* 25, no. 3 (1997): 347–76.

12. In chapter 5 I consider this type of criticism at the level of practice to analyze whether more contestatory, rights-based education advocacy can be squared with deliberative norms.

13. See Clarissa Rile Hayward, "Doxa and Deliberation," *Critical Review of International Social and Political Philosophy* 7, no. 1 (2004): 1–24.

14. For example, Jürgen Habermas treats basic welfare rights as a prerequisite to legitimate deliberations but does not give education sustained treatment. See Habermas, *Between Facts and Norms: Contributions to a Discourse Theory of Law and Democracy*, trans. William Rehg (Cambridge, MA: MIT Press, 1996). James Bohman briefly mentions how educational institutions must prepare citizens to deliberate as political equals, but does not elaborate on what this requirement entails or what it means for the scope of democratic authority over education policy. See Bohman, "Deliberative Democracy and Effective Social Freedom: Capabilities, Resources, and Opportunities," in *Deliberative Democracy: Essays on Reason and Politics*, ed. James Bohman and William Rehg (Cambridge, MA: MIT Press, 2002), especially 332 and 345.

15. Gutmann and Thompson, *Democracy and Disagreement*, 66.

16. Joshua Cohen similarly argues that deliberative theory can overcome the tension between procedural and substantive equality; see Cohen, "Procedure and Substance in Deliberative Democracy," in *Deliberative Democracy: Essays on Reason and Politics*, ed. James Bohman and William Rehg (Cambridge, MA: MIT Press, 2002), 407–37. I focus on Gutmann and Thompson's theory because they directly address policy questions about basic social goods like education.

17. Gutmann and Thompson, *Democracy and Disagreement*, 27.

18. Ibid., 211–15.

19. Ibid., 273.

20. Amy Gutmann, *Democratic Education* (Princeton: Princeton University Press, 1999), 136.

21. Ibid., 137.

22. Randall Curren similarly questions Gutmann's logic of deferring to majoritarian deliberations to determine the content of the democratic standard for education; see Curren, *Aristotle on the Necessity of Public Education* (Lanham, MD: Rowman and Littlefield, 2000), 191.

23. Gutmann and Thompson, *Democracy and Disagreement*, 201–9.

24. Gary Orfield, John Kucsera, and Genevieve Siegel-Hawley, *E Pluribus . . . Separation: Deepening Double Segregation for More Students* (Los Angeles: The Civil Rights Project/Proyecto Derechos Civiles, 2012), 19, 36.

25. Ibid., 26.

26. Joshua Cohen, "Deliberation and Democratic Legitimacy," in *Deliberative Democracy: Essays on Reason and Politics*, ed. James Bohman and William Rehg (Cambridge, MA: MIT Press, 2002), 74.

27. Ian Shapiro makes a similar point in his criticism of Gutmann and Thompson's deliberative theory; see Shapiro, "Enough of Deliberation: Politics Is about Interests and Power," in *Deliberative Politics: Essays on Democracy and Disagreement*, ed. Stephen Macedo (New York: Oxford University Press, 1999), 33–34.

28. Bohman, "Deliberative Democracy," 336.

29. San Antonio Independent School District v. Rodriguez, 411 U.S. 1 (1973). I discuss this case in chapter 3.

30. Ibid., at 113.

31. Interview with Catherine Lhamon, former racial justice director, American Civil Liberties Union of Southern California, March 14, 2007.

32. Ian Shapiro, *The State of Democratic Theory* (Princeton, NJ: Princeton University Press, 2003), 133.

33. For a summary of the benefits that research indicates are attached to educational attainment, see William S. Koski and Rob Reich, "When 'Adequate' Isn't: The Retreat from Equity in Educational Law and Policy and Why It Matters," *Emory Law Journal* 56, no. 3 (2006): 599–602.

34. Gutmann and Thompson, *Democracy and Disagreement*, 36.

35. Harry Brighouse, *School Choice and Social Justice* (Oxford: Oxford University Press, 2000), 56.

36. Fung, *Empowered Participation*.

37. Ibid., 111–16.

38. Susan Ryan et al., *Charting Reform: LSCs — Local Leadership at Work* (Chicago: Consortium on Chicago School Research, 1997), cited in Fung, *Empowered Participation*, 116.

39. Fung, *Empowered Participation*, 116.

40. Ryan et al., *Charting Reform*, 10–11.

41. Schools were considered integrated if more than 30 percent of their student body was white. Ibid., 11.

42. Lorraine M. McDonnell and M. Stephen Weatherford, *Practical Deliberation in Local School Districts: A South Carolina Experiment* (Los Angeles: Center for the Study of Evaluation, University of California–Los Angeles, 2000), 20–22; see also M. Stephen Weatherford and Lorraine McDonnell, "Deliberation with a Purpose: Reconnecting Communities and Schools," in *Deliberation, Participation and Democracy: Can the People Govern?* ed. Shawn W. Rosenberg (New York: Palgrave Macmillan, 2007).

43. McDonnell and Weatherford, *Practical Deliberation*, 20–22.

44. Shapiro, "Enough of Deliberation," 34.

45. Of course, educational attainment affects citizens' political engagement across a range of activities, including voting, protesting, and letter writing. I focus on the inequalities that arise in deliberative forums not because deliberation is necessarily less egalitarian than other forms of political participation, but to highlight how it is less egalitarian than theory suggests when it comes to making education policy.

CHAPTER TWO

1. In this chapter, I use rights to mean moral entitlements that are central to a just society of political equals. This usage is more inclusive than the narrower category of legal rights, on which I focus in chapter 4 when I consider court-based education reform.

2. Several educational theorists have recently taken up the issue of a right to education; see Michael S. Katz, "Is There a Right to Education? A Philosophical Analysis through U.S. Lenses," in *Education, Democracy, and the Moral Life*, ed. Michael S. Katz, Susan Verducci, and Gert Biesta (New York: Springer, 2008); and Randall Curren, "Education as a Social Right in a Diverse Society," *Journal of Philosophy of Education* 43, no. 1 (2009): 45–56. But neither of these essays considers at length the tension between rights claims and democratic authority.

3. See Eamonn Callan, *Creating Citizens: Political Education and Liberal Democracy* (Oxford: Oxford University Press, 1997); Meira Levinson, *The Demands of Liberal Education* (Oxford: Oxford University Press, 1999); and Rob Reich, *Bridging Liberalism and Multiculturalism in American Education* (Chicago: University of Chicago Press, 2002).

4. A possible counterpoint to my focus on citizenship would be to consider educational rights targeted at preparing students for the labor market. I do not address this because I find that it provides too anemic a conception of education at a time when policy debates focus overwhelming on the economic returns to education, at the expense of concern for the role of education in a viable, participatory democracy.

5. Jeremy Waldron notes that this is the primary concern of political theorists, while political philosophers focus on the tension between individual rights and utilitarian theory. See Waldron, *Liberal Rights: Collected Papers, 1981–1991* (Cambridge: Cambridge University Press, 1993), 392–421.

6. I draw heavily on Jeremy Waldron's survey of this typology; see Waldron, "Rights," in *A Companion to Contemporary Political Philosophy*, ed. Robert E. Goodin and Philip Pettit (Oxford, Blackwell, 1993), 578–81.

7. Ibid., 579.

8. See Stephen Holmes and Cass Sunstein, *The Cost of Rights: Why Liberty Depends on Taxes* (New York: W. W. Norton, 1999).

9. Waldron, "Rights," 578–80.

10. Nozick writes: "No one has a right to something whose realization requires certain uses of things and activities that other people have rights and entitlements over. . . . The particular rights over things fill the space of rights, leaving no room for general rights to be in a certain material condition." See Nozick, *Anarchy, State, and Utopia* (New York: Basic Books, 1974), 238.

11. Maurice Cranston, "Are There Any Human Rights?" *Daedalus* 112, no. 4 (1983): 12.

12. This contrasts with some constitutions drafted more recently (for example, in India and South Africa), which enumerate positive rights to housing, employment, and education. For an international comparative analysis of constitutional support for welfare rights, see Cass R. Sunstein, *The Second Bill of Rights: FDR's Unfinished Revolution and Why We Need It More Than Ever* (New York: Basic Books, 2004), 104.

13. For a classic defense of socioeconomic rights in legal theory, see Frank I. Michel-

man, "Foreword: On Protecting the Poor through the Fourteenth Amendment," *Harvard Law Review* 83, no. 7 (1969): 7–59.

14. Mary Ann Glendon, *Rights Talk: The Impoverishment of Political Discourse* (New York: Free Press, 1991), 41.

15. Waldron, *Liberal Rights*, 353–57.

16. Human rights are another category of rights that arise across all three generations of rights. Because they are universal rights, they are typically expressed in very general terms. The United Nations' Universal Declaration of Human Rights, for example, says: "Education shall be free, at least in the elementary and fundamental stages. . . . It shall promote understanding, tolerance." The right to education that I defend is compatible with these goals but is more narrowly tailored to a deliberative democracy. See United Nations General Assembly, *Universal Declaration of Human Rights*, December 10, 1948, http://www.un.org/Overview/rights.html.

17. See Philippe Van Parijs, *Real Freedom for All* (Oxford: Clarendon, 1995); Philippe Van Parijs, "Why Surfers Should Be Fed: The Liberal Case for an Unconditional Basic Income," *Philosophy and Public Affairs* 20, no. 2 (1991): 101–31. For essays on basic income and basic capital, see Keith Dowding, Jurgen De Wispelaere, and Stuart White, eds., *The Ethics of Stakeholding* (New York: Palgrave Macmillan, 2003); for entitlements to health care, see Norman Daniels, *Just Health Care* (Cambridge: Cambridge University Press, 1985).

18. See Waldron, *Liberal Rights*, 276.

19. Lesley A. Jacobs, *Rights and Deprivation* (Oxford: Oxford University Press, 1993), 186–87.

20. For example, Henry Shue argues that though education yields "greater and richer enjoyment," a right to education must give way to rights to physical security if a tradeoff is unavoidable; he thus concentrates his analysis on security and subsistence rights. See Shue, *Basic Rights: Subsistence, Affluence, and U.S. Foreign Policy* (Princeton, NJ: Princeton University Press, 1980), 20.

21. Carole Pateman, "Freedom and Democratization: Why Basic Income Is to Be Preferred to Basic Capital," in *The Ethics of Stakeholding*, ed. Keith Dowding, Jurgen De Wispelaere, and Stuart White (New York: Palgrave Macmillan, 2003), 131–32.

22. T. H. Marshall, "Citizenship and Social Class," in *Class, Citizenship, and Social Development: Essays by T. H. Marshall* (Garden City, NY: Doubleday and Company, 1964), 65–122.

23. Corey Brettschneider, *Democratic Rights: The Substance of Self-Government* (Princeton, NJ: Princeton University Press, 2007). In a separate article I extend Brettschneider's theory to educational rights; see Anne Newman, "A Democratic Framework for Educational Rights," *Educational Theory* 62, no. 1 (2012): 7–23.

24. For a summary of the economic benefits that are correlated with education, as part of their argument for why education is a positional good, see William S. Koski and Rob Reich, "When 'Adequate' Isn't: The Retreat from Equity in Educational Law and Policy and Why It Matters," *Emory Law Journal* 56, no. 3 (2006): 600–603.

25. See Brettschneider, *Democratic Rights*, 13–15.

26. See Norman H. Nie, Jane Junn, and Kenneth Stehlik-Barry, *Education and Democratic Citizenship in America* (Chicago: University of Chicago Press, 1996); and Sidney

Verba, Kay Lehman Schlozman, and Henry E. Brady, *Voice and Equality: Civic Voluntarism in American Politics* (Cambridge, MA: Harvard University Press, 1995).

27. Amartya Sen, "Equality of What?" The Tanner Lecture on Human Values, Stanford University, May 22, 1979, http://www.tannerlectures.utah.edu/lectures/documents/sen80.pdf.

28. On the connection between poverty and educational achievement, see David Berliner, "Our Impoverished View of Educational Research," *Teachers College Record* 108, no. 6 (2006): 949–95.

29. On the multiple and competing interpretations of equality of educational opportunity, see Christopher Jencks, "Whom Must We Treat Equally for Educational Opportunity to Be Equal?" *Ethics* 98, no. 3 (1988): 518–33.

30. For example, see Elizabeth Anderson, "Rethinking Equality of Opportunity: Comment on Adam Swift's *How Not to Be a Hypocrite*," *Theory and Research in Education* 2, no. 2 (2004): 99–110, and Debra Satz, "Equality, Adequacy and Education for Citizenship," *Ethics* 117, no. 4 (2007): 623–48. One exception is Harry Brighouse, who argues that democracy should not be the principle value that guides education policy making because it may not lead to just outcomes that advance children's educational interests. He thus briefly endorses the notion of a right to education, but a rights framework is not central to his analysis. See Brighouse, *School Choice and Social Justice* (Oxford: Oxford University Press, 2000), 61–63.

31. Aristotle, *The Politics*, trans. and ed. Ernest Barker (London: Oxford University Press, 1958), 333 (1337a).

32. Benjamin Rush, "Thoughts upon the Mode of Education Proper in a Republic," in *Essays on Education in the Early Republic*, ed. Frederick Rudolph (Cambridge, MA: Belknap, 1965), 13–14.

33. John Rawls, *Political Liberalism* (New York: Columbia University Press, 1996), 375.

34. For attention to these questions and their bearing on education, see Callan, *Creating Citizens*; Levinson, *Demands of Liberal Education*; and Reich, *Bridging Liberalism*.

35. Rawls presumes that political autonomy for individuals' use in the public sphere can be neatly distinguished from a more encompassing personal autonomy that would shape individuals' choices in the private sphere. The plausibility of this distinction is highly questionable; see Callan, *Creating Citizens*, chapter 2.

36. Ibid., 199.

37. Callan, *Creating Citizens*, 50. Callan's broader point is that Rawls's exclusion of autonomy from civic education renders his political liberalism untenable and that the sharp contrast Rawls draws between comprehensive and political liberalism falls apart upon closer inspection. See *Creating Citizens*, 39–42.

38. See Callan, *Creating Citizens*; Levinson, *Demands of Liberal Education*; Reich, *Bridging Liberalism*.

39. William Galston, *Liberal Purposes: Goods, Virtues, and Diversity in the Liberal State* (Cambridge: Cambridge University Press, 1991), 254.

40. Eamonn Callan, "Galston's Dilemma and *Wisconsin v. Yoder*," *Theory and Research in Education* 4, no. 3 (2006): 264.

41. Richard Arneson and Ian Shapiro, "Democratic Autonomy and Religious Freedom: A Critique of *Wisconsin v. Yoder*," in *Political Order: Nomos XXXVIII*, ed. Ian Shapiro and Russell Hardin (New York: New York University Press, 1996), 398.

42. On how public deliberations can influence individuals' internalized deliberations about how to vote, see Robert Goodin, *Reflective Democracy* (Oxford: Oxford University Press, 2003).

43. For extended treatment of this tension in liberalism and multicultural theory, see Reich, *Bridging Liberalism and Multiculturalism in American Education*.

44. See Callan, *Creating Citizens*; Reich, *Bridging Liberalism*; Levinson, *Demands of Liberal Education*; and Ian MacMullen, *Faith in Schools?* (Princeton, NJ: Princeton University Press, 2007). One exception to most theorists' focus on whether an autonomy-promoting education can be squared with liberalism's commitment to diversity is Richard Dagger's view of autonomy, which centers on its implications for political participation from a civic republican perspective. Yet Dagger's primary aim is to reconcile liberalism and republicanism, so the issue of political equality does not have a central role in his analysis. See Dagger, *Civic Virtues: Rights, Citizenship, and Republican Liberalism* (Oxford: Oxford University Press, 1997).

45. Gutmann, "Civic Education and Social Diversity" *Ethics* 105, no. 3 (1995): 573.

46. Theorists' language is often weaker on this point than rights discourse; for example, Rob Reich writes that the state "*can* set as a fundamental aim of education the development of autonomy"; see Reich, *Bridging Liberalism*, 112 (italics in the original).

47. John Rawls, *A Theory of Justice*, rev. ed. (Cambridge, MA: Harvard University Press, 1999), 366. Meira Levinson makes a compelling argument that Rawls's concern for individuals' capacity to develop and revise their conception of the good requires individual autonomy, not just political autonomy; see Levinson, *Demands of Liberal Education*, 19–21.

48. Ibid., 366–367.

49. Ibid., 366.

50. Amy Gutmann and Dennis Thompson, *Democracy and Disagreement* (Cambridge, MA: Belknap, 1996), 79.

51. One exception is Nie, Junn, and Stehlik-Barry, *Education and Democratic Citizenship*, in which the authors define their understanding of political engagement as being "close to the notion of autonomy, understood as authorship of one's life in the social context, with a bundling of identity and interest, where people are capable of choosing their own actions" (16).

52. Robert Putnam, quoted in Thomas S. Dee, "Are There Civic Returns to Education?," *Journal of Public Economics* 88 (2004): 1700.

53. For voting data, see ibid., 1709; for data on support for free speech, see ibid., 1716. On the latter point, Dee found that individuals' support for the free speech rights of homosexuals, communists, and antireligionists strongly increased with years of schooling, but this correlation did not hold for the speech rights of militarists and racists; see ibid., 1716–717.

54. Samuel L. Popkin and Michael A. Dimock, "Political Knowledge and Citizen Competence," in *Citizen Competence and Democratic Institutions*, ed. Stephen L. Elkin and Karol Edward Soltan (University Park, PA: Pennsylvania State University Press,

1999), 117–46. Galston's helpful review article on empirical studies of civic information, education, and participation pointed me to this work; see Galston, "Political Knowledge, Political Engagement, and Civic Education," *Annual Review of Political Science* 4 (2001): 217–34.

55. Levinson, *Demands of Liberal Education*, 103.

56. Norman Nie and D. Sunshine Hillygus, "Education and Democratic Citizenship," in *Making Good Citizens: Education and Civil Society*, ed. Diane Ravitch and Joseph P. Viteritti (New Haven, CT: Yale University Press, 2001), 42. This study found that mathematical aptitude may have a slight negative correlation with civic participation.

57. For analysis of this case, and more broadly the skills necessary for civic participation that are addressed in school finance litigation, see Michael Rebell, "Adequacy Litigations: A New Path to Equity?" in *Bringing Equity Back: Research for a New Era in American Educational Policy*, ed. Janice Petrovich and Amy Stuart Wells (New York: Teachers College Press, 2005), 302–7.

58. Rose v. Council for Better Education, 790 S.W. 2d 186 (1989).

59. Callan, *Creating Citizens*, 113–14.

60. William Galston, "Civic Education in the Liberal State," in *Philosophers on Education: New Historical Perspectives*, ed. Amelie Oksenberg Rorty (London: Routledge, 1998), 470–80.

61. Callan, *Creating Citizens*, 114.

62. Ibid., 115.

63. Rawls, *Political Liberalism*, 213.

64. Gutmann and Thompson, *Democracy and Disagreement*, 53. Reciprocity and accountability are central principles in Gutmann and Thompson's deliberative theory; see 52–94 and 128–64.

65. Ibid., 360.

66. Rawls, *Political Liberalism*, 251.

67. Gutmann and Thompson, *Democracy and Disagreement*, 132–37.

68. This argument for condoning departures from public reason in unjust times is central to Archon Fung's support of deliberative activism "before the revolution." See Fung, "Deliberation before the Revolution: Toward an Ethics of Deliberative Democracy in an Unjust World," *Political Theory* 33, no. 2 (2005): 397–419. I consider his argument in chapter 5 when analyzing one advocacy organization's education reform campaigns.

69. Dee, "Are There Civic Returns to Education?," 1716–17.

70. Michael X. Delli Carpini and Scott Keeter, *What Americans Know about Politics and Why It Matters* (New Haven, CT: Yale University Press, 1996), 259–60, cited in Galston, "Political Knowledge, Political Engagement, and Civic Education."

71. Nie and Hillygus, "Education and Democratic Citizenship," 44–46. This study found that having more college credits in science and engineering may have a slightly negative impact on students' desire for political influence, while having more credits in business is connected with "very strong proclivities to avoid the public and embrace the attainment of wealth" (45).

72. Nie, June, and Stehlik-Barry, *Education and Democratic Citizenship in America*, 11–38.

73. Waldron, *Liberal Rights*, 215.

CHAPTER THREE

1. Maurice Cranston, "Are There Any Human Rights?" *Daedalus* 112, no. 4 (1983): 13.

2. Amartya Sen argues this point with respect to human rights; see Sen, "Elements of a Theory of Human Rights," *Philosophy and Public Affairs* 32, no. 4 (2004): 347–48.

3. Jennifer Hochschild and Nathan Scovronick, *The American Dream and the Public Schools* (Oxford: Oxford University Press, 2003), 9.

4. Cass R. Sunstein, *The Second Bill of Rights: FDR's Unfinished Revolution and Why We Need It More than Ever* (New York: Basic Books, 2004).

5. San Antonio Independent School District v. Rodriguez, 411 U.S. 1 (1973).

6. Bruce Ackerman identifies these three periods as "constitutional moments" during which the Constitution took on new meaning either through the legislative process or because a majority of citizens were politically engaged and mobilized by catalyzing events. See Ackerman, *We the People: Foundations* (Cambridge, MA: Belknap, 1991). Cass Sunstein similarly identifies these three periods as sources of deliberative democracy in the United States; see Sunstein, *The Partial Constitution* (Cambridge, MA: Harvard University Press, 1993), 134.

7. Jeannie Oakes and colleagues offer a shorter historical survey of the status of a right to education in the United States that covers some similar and some different ground; see Jeannie Oakes, John Rogers, Gary Blasi, and Martin Lipton, "Grassroots Organizing, Social Movements, and the Right to High-Quality Education," *Stanford Journal of Civil Rights and Civil Liberties* 4, no. 2 (2008): 342–48.

8. Carl F. Kaestle, "Equal Educational Opportunity and the Federal Government: A Response to Goodwin Liu," *Yale Law Journal Pocket Part* 116, no. 152 (2006).

9. Gordon S. Wood, *The Creation of the American Republic, 1776–1787* (Chapel Hill: University of North Carolina Press, 1998), 47.

10. Moses Mather, *America's Appeal to the Imperial World* (1775), quoted in ibid., 120.

11. Benjamin Rush, "Thoughts upon the Mode of Education Proper in a Republic," in *Essays on Education in the Early Republic*, ed. Frederick Rudolph (Cambridge, MA: Belknap, 1965), 10.

12. For a comparison of the educational theories of Rush, Webster, and Jefferson, see David B. Tyack, ed., *Turning Points in American Educational History* (Waltham, MA: Blaisdell, 1967), 83–118.

13. Samuel Harrison Smith, "Remarks on Education" (1797), quoted in Carl F. Kaestle, *Pillars of the Republic: Common Schools and American Society, 1780–1860* (New York: Hill and Wang, 1983), 7.

14. James Madison quoted in Ellwood P. Cubberley, *Public Education in the United States: A Study and Interpretation of American Educational History* (Cambridge, MA: Riverside, 1947), 90.

15. Sunstein, *Partial Constitution*; also Joseph M. Bessette, *The Mild Voice of Reason: Deliberative Democracy and American National Government* (Chicago: University of Chicago Press, 1994); and Christopher L. Eisgruber, *Constitutional Self-Government* (Cambridge, MA: Harvard University Press, 2001).

16. There are a variety of explanations for why education does not appear in the

U.S. Constitution. Ellwood Cubberley suggests that it is absent because education had been privately managed (mainly by religious institutions), so there was no precedent for making it a state responsibility. He also notes that the participants in the Constitutional Convention had many significant problems on their agenda, and accordingly set aside issues like education. See Cubberley, *Public Education*, 85–86. Other reasons include the fact that the Constitution is a charter of negative liberties rather than positive ones, and framers' concern for preserving states' rights and local control.

17. Wood, *Creation of the American Republic*, 413–17.

18. Ibid., 402–3; also J. A. Pocock, *The Machiavellian Moment* (Princeton, NJ: Princeton University Press, 1975), 506–52.

19. Wood, *Creation of the American Republic*, 415.

20. Thomas Jefferson, "A Bill for the More General Diffusion of Knowledge," in *The Educational Works of Thomas Jefferson*, ed. Roy J. Honeywell (Cambridge, MA: Harvard University Press, 1931), 199.

21. Richard D. Brown, *The Strength of a People: The Idea of an Informed Citizenry in America, 1650–1870* (Chapel Hill: University of North Carolina Press, 1996), 92.

22. Lorraine Smith Pangle and Thomas L. Pangle, *The Learning of Liberty: The Educational Ideas of the American Founders* (Lawrence: University Press of Kansas, 1993), 151.

23. Kaestle, *Pillars*, 9–10.

24. I am indebted to Goodwin Liu's analysis of reform proposals from the Reconstruction period, which brought to my attention highly relevant congressional debates about national citizenship and the federal role in public education; see Liu, "Education, Equality, and National Citizenship," *Yale Law Journal* 116, no. 2 (2006): 367–99.

25. Tyack, *Turning Points*, 120.

26. Liu, "Education, Equality," 372–75.

27. Representative Moulton, 39th Congress, 1st Sess., 1867, *Congressional Globe*, Part 4, 3045. Part of this quote appears in Liu, "Education, Equality."

28. Representative Ignatius Donnelly, who introduced the 1865 bill to establish the Department of Education; quoted in Liu, "Education, Equality," 373.

29. Liu, "Education, Equality," 376.

30. Ibid., 376–77.

31. Statement of Representative George Frisbie Hoar to 42nd Congress, 1871, quoted in Liu, "Education, Equality," 380.

32. Statement of Senator Henry William Blair (1884), quoted in Liu, "Education, Equality," 389.

33. David Tyack, Thomas James, and Aaron Benavot, *Law and the Shaping of Public Education, 1785–1954* (Madison: University of Wisconsin Press, 1987), 55–57 and 143–45.

34. Sunstein, *Second Bill of Rights*, 9–34.

35. Franklin D. Roosevelt, "Message to the Congress on the State of the Union," January 11, 1944, in *The Public Papers and Addresses of Franklin D. Roosevelt*, vol. 13, ed. Samuel I. Rosenman (New York: Harper and Brothers, 1950), 41.

36. Ibid., 40–41.

37. Ibid., 41.

38. See Sunstein, *Partial Constitution*; Larry Kramer, *The People Themselves: Popular Constitutionalism and Judicial Review* (New York: Oxford University Press, 2004); and Ackerman, *We the People: Foundations*. For a classic statement on judicial review that argues for a limited set of judicially enforced rights, see John Hart Ely, *Democracy and Distrust: A Theory of Judicial Review* (Cambridge, MA: Harvard University Press, 1980). For a more expansive view of the rights that the judiciary should enforce because of moral considerations, see Ronald Dworkin, *Taking Rights Seriously* (Cambridge, MA: Harvard University Press, 1977).

39. Sunstein, *Second Bill of Rights*.

40. Randy E. Barnett and Cass R. Sunstein, "Constitutive Commitments and Roosevelt's Second Bill of Rights: A Dialogue," *Drake Law Review* 53, no. 2 (2005): 217.

41. Sunstein, *Partial Constitution*.

42. William E. Forbath, "Why Is This Rights Talk Different from All Other Rights Talk? Demoting the Court and Reimagining the Constitution," review of *The Partial Constitution*, by Cass Sunstein, *Stanford Law Review* 46, no. 6 (1994): 1774.

43. For a positive appraisal of the New Deal's legacy, see Bruce Ackerman, *We the People: Transformations* (Cambridge, MA: Belknap, 1998).For a more skeptical view and critique of Ackerman's arguments, see William E. Forbath, "Constitutional Change and the Politics of History," *Yale Law Journal* 108, no. 8 (1999): 1927–930.

44. James MacGregor Burns, quoted in David M. Kennedy, *Freedom from Fear: The American People in Depression and War, 1929–1945* (New York: Oxford University Press, 1999).

45. This figure was calculated in 2006 dollars; see Michael Heise, "The Story of *San Antonio Independent School Dist. v. Rodriguez*: School Finance, Local Control, and Constitutional Limits," Cornell Law Faculty Publications, Paper 76 (2007): 3, http://scholarship.law.cornell.edu/lsrp_papers/76.

46. Ibid.

47. Rodriguez v. San Antonio Independent School District, 337 F. Supp. 280 (W.D. Tex., 1972).

48. The Court denied that wealth counts as a suspect classification, in contrast to race or nationality, which it does recognize in this way.

49. The following analysis builds on my arguments in "Transforming a Moral Right into a Legal Right: The Case of School Finance Litigation and the Right to Education," in *Philosophy of Education Yearbook 2006*, ed. Daniel Vokey (Urbana, IL: Philosophy of Education Society), 82–90.

50. John E. Coons, William H. Clune III, and Stephen D. Sugarman, *Private Wealth and Public Education* (Cambridge, MA: Belknap, 1970).

51. Coons, Clune, and Sugarman located their alternative funding scheme at the state level to even out resources between districts. They argued: "The quality of public education may not be a function of wealth other than the wealth of the state as a whole." See Coons, Clune, and Sugarman, *Private Wealth*, 2. This strategy is less radical than present-day calls to equalize spending across states because of vast interstate inequalities, which Liu argues are now greater than intrastate inequalities. See Liu, "National Citizenship and the Promise of Equal Educational Opportunity," *Yale Law Journal Pocket Part* 116, no. 145 (2006), http://www.yalelawjournal.org/images/pdfs/77.pdf. Nonetheless,

establishment of the principle of fiscal neutrality was a significant step toward breaking the link between class and educational opportunity.

52. Coons, Clune, and Sugarman, *Private Wealth*, 7.

53. The Supreme Court had found in favor of indigent criminal defendants who argued that they were entitled to free court transcripts in *Griffin v. Illinois*, 351 U.S. 12 (1956); it also banned incarceration as a penalty for inability to pay a fine in *Williams v. Illinois*, 399 U.S. 235 (1970), and in *Tate v. Short*, 401 U.S. 395 (1971).

54. Peter B. Edelman, "The Next Century of Our Constitution: Rethinking Our Duty to the Poor," *Hastings Law Journal* 39, no.1 (1987): 34.

55. Frank I. Michelman, "Foreword: On Protecting the Poor through the Fourteenth Amendment," *Harvard Law Review* 83, no.7 (1969): 7–59.

56. Ibid., 59.

57. Brief for Appellees, *San Antonio Independent School District v. Rodriguez*, 411 U.S. 1 (1973), at 31–32.

58. Ibid., at 37.

59. Ibid.

60. See Papsan v. Allain, 478 U.S. 265 (1986), and the dissenting opinion to Kadrmas v. Dickinson Public Schools, 487 U.S. 450 (1988). For discussion of these cases in relation to *Rodriguez* and a minimal right to education, see Mark G. Yudof, David K. Kirp, Betsy Levin, and Rachel F. Moran, *Educational Policy and the Law*, 4th ed. (Belmont, CA: Thomson Learning, 2002), 796. This interpretation of *Rodriguez* is also discussed in Sunstein, *Second Bill of Rights*, 166, and Peter Edelman uses the open possibility of a right to an adequate education to argue for a right to a basic income; see Edelman, "Next Century," 34.

61. *San Antonio Independent School District*, 411 U.S. 1 (1973), at 37.

62. Ibid., at 36.

63. Marshall emphasizes this point in his dissenting opinion; see ibid., at 115–16.

64. To make this point, the Court distinguished its recent decisions that protected the rights of indigents in other arenas from the facts of the *Rodriguez* case. The Court argued that the burdens on the poor in these previous cases amounted to complete deprivation of certain benefits, whereas the Edgewood students were not completely denied an education; see *San Antonio Independent School District*, 411 U.S. 1 (1973), at 20–25. In a much-discussed footnote, the majority decision does acknowledge that the Court would likely take a different view if it were presented with a case in which students had to pay tuition to access public education; see *San Antonio Independent School District*, 411 U.S. 1 (1973), at 25.

65. *San Antonio Independent School District*, 411 U.S. 1 (1973), at 71.

66. Ibid., at 112.

67. Ibid., at 98–99.

68. Ibid., at 103.

69. Ibid., at 126.

70. Ibid., at 89.

71. William S. Koski and Rob Reich, "When 'Adequate' Isn't: The Retreat from Equity in Educational Law and Policy and Why It Matters," *Emory Law Journal* 56, no. 3 (2006): 545–617.

72. See Elizabeth Anderson, "Rethinking Equality of Opportunity: Comment on Adam Swift's *How Not to Be a Hypocrite*," *Theory and Research in Education* 2, no. 2 (2004): 99–110; also see Debra Satz, "Equality, Adequacy and Education for Citizenship," *Ethics* 117, no. 4 (2007): 623–48.

73. Koski and Reich, "When 'Adequate' Isn't," 599–603.

74. Anderson, "Rethinking Equality of Opportunity," 105.

75. Harry Brighouse and Adam Swift, "Educational Equality versus Educational Adequacy: A Critique of Anderson and Satz," *Journal of Applied Philosophy* 26, no. 2 (2009): 120.

76. Koski and Reich, "When 'Adequate' Isn't," 606–7.

77. Satz, "Equality, Adequacy and Education for Citizenship," 635–39.

78. Liu, "Education, Equality, and National Citizenship," 346.

79. Satz, "Equality, Adequacy and Education for Citizenship"; Anderson, "Rethinking Equality of Opportunity," 107–9.

80. Arne Duncan, "The Well-Rounded Curriculum," speech at the Arts Education Partnership National Forum, April 9, 2010, http://www2.ed.gov/news/speeches/2010/04/04092010.html. Representative Jesse Jackson Jr. of Illinois introduced a constitutional amendment to make education a federal right in 2003. The Southern Education Foundation has also called for a constitutional amendment to ensure that all students receive an equal, high-quality public education; see Southern Education Foundation, *No Time to Lose: Why America Needs an Education Amendment to the US Constitution to Improve Public Education* (Atlanta: Southern Education Foundation, 2009).

CHAPTER FOUR

1. William M. Beckner, speaking at the 1890 Kentucky Constitutional Convention, quoted in a brief of amici curiae for *Rose v. Council for Better Education* by the Prichard Committee for Academic Excellence and Kentuckians for the Commonwealth.

2. Brief for appellees, *Rose v. Council for Better Education*, November 28, 1988, p. 1.

3. On the growth of community organizing for education reform, see Dennis Shirley, "Community Organizing and Educational Change: A Reconnaissance," *Journal of Educational Change* 10, nos. 2–3 (2009): 229–37. For current information on school funding litigation across the United States, see the website maintained by National Education Access Network, based at Teachers College, Columbia University: http://www.schoolfunding.info.

4. Jeremy Waldron, *Liberal Rights: Collected Papers, 1981–1991* (Cambridge: Cambridge University Press, 1993), 31–32.

5. Rose v. Council for Better Education, 790 S.W. 2d 186 (1989).

6. When Guess began organizing support for a lawsuit, he had recently been fired from his Department of Education position for political reasons; see Matthew H. Bosworth, *Courts as Catalysts: State Supreme Courts and Public School Finance Equity* (Albany, NY: SUNY Press, 2001), 115–16.

7. Memorandum dated April 12, 1984 (on file with author).

8. Brief for Appellees, *Rose v. Council for Better Education*, November 28, 1988, p. 1–2.

9. Several interviewees used this phrase when discussing the conditions of education in Kentucky, including Justin Bathon, Assistant Professor, University of Kentucky College of Education, October 13, 2011; Richard Day, Assistant Professor, Eastern Kentucky University College of Education, October 17, 2011; David Karem, former Kentucky State Senator, November 18, 2011.

10. This was Bert Combs's reaction to the decision as recalled by Debra Dawahare, Combs's co-counsel; interview with Dawahare, October 20, 2011.

11. State courts that have drawn from the *Rose* decision include those in Massachusetts, Alabama, New Hampshire, North Carolina, and South Carolina; see Molly A. Hunter, "All Eyes Forward: Public Engagement and Educational Reform in Kentucky," *Journal of Law and Education* 28, no. 4 (1999): 487n70.

12. For example, see Peter Enrich, "Leaving Equality Behind: New Directions in School Finance Reform," *Vanderbilt Law Review* 48, no. 101 (1995): 101–94; William S. Koski, "Of Fuzzy Standards and Institutional Constraints: A Re-Examination of the Jurisprudential History of Educational Finance Reform Litigation," *Santa Clara Law Review* 43, no. 4 (2003): 1185–298; Michael Heise, "State Constitutions, School Finance Litigation, and the 'Third Wave': From Equity to Adequacy," *Temple Law Review* 68 (1995): 1151–76.

13. Memo from Council for Better Education Steering Committee, May 14, 1984 (on file with author).

14. Bert T. Combs, "Creative Constitutional Law: The Kentucky School Reform Law," *Harvard Journal on Legislation* 28 (1991): 369.

15. Combs took the case on a pro bono basis, but the Council for Better Education had other fees to pay associated with the lawsuit. It thus assessed each participating district $0.50 per pupil on the basis of average daily attendance; interview with Jack Moreland, former president of the Council for Better Education, October 24, 2011.

16. For a history of the Prichard Committee and its approach to reform, written by its first executive director, see Robert F. Sexton, *Mobilizing Citizens for Better Schools* (New York: Teachers College Press, 2004).

17. Ronald G. Dove, "Acorns in a Mountain Pool: The Role of Litigation, Law, and Lawyers in Kentucky Education Reform," *Journal of Education Finance* 17, no. 1 (1991): 110; Dove also discusses Edward Prichard Jr.'s rise and then fall after he was caught stuffing ballot boxes, which prompted his drive to redeem his reputation in Kentucky politics.

18. "Report on Town Forums in Kentucky," compiled by Scottie Kenkel, edited by Steve Kay and Rona Roberts, for the Prichard Committee for Academic Excellence in 1985.

19. Interview with Jack Moreland, October 24, 2011.

20. Interview with Richard Day, October 17, 2011.

21. Interview with Cindy Heine, associate executive director and former interim director of the Prichard Committee for Academic Excellence, October 28, 2011.

22. Interview with Diana Taylor, former chief of staff to Kentucky governor Brereton Jones, November 8, 2011.

23. William L. F. Felstiner, Richard L. Abel, and Austin Sarat, "The Emergence and Transformation of Disputes: Naming, Blaming, Claiming," *Law and Society Review* 15, nos. 3/4 (1980–81): 631–54.

24. For a seminal study of legal advocacy and social change that documents the challenges and benefits of legal mobilization, see Michael McCann, *Rights at Work: Pay Equity Reform and the Politics of Legal Mobilization* (Chicago: University of Chicago Press, 1994).

25. Stuart A. Scheingold, *The Politics of Rights: Lawyers, Public Policy, and Political Change*, 2nd ed. (Ann Arbor: University of Michigan Press, 2004), 132–34.

26. Interview with Jack Moreland, October 24, 2011.

27. Interview with Diana Taylor, November 8, 2011.

28. On the media's role in the *Rose* litigation and subsequent reforms, see Bosworth, *Courts as Catalysts*, 144–45

29. Interview with Cindy Heine, October 28, 2011.

30. Interview with David Karem, November 18, 2011.

31. The Council for Better Education's case did include a handful of student plaintiffs, but the Council focused on superintendents largely because they could raise money through their districts to fund the legal effort; interview with Theodore Lavit, co-counsel for *Rose* plaintiffs, December 2, 2011.

32. C. Scott Trimble and Andrew C. Forsaith, "Achieving Equity and Excellence in KY Education," *University of Michigan Journal of Law Reform* 28 no. 3 (1994–1995): 605.

33. Section 183 of the Kentucky Constitution reads as follows: "The General Assembly shall, by appropriate legislation, provide for an efficient system of common schools throughout the State."

34. See Combs, "Creative Constitutional Law," 371–72.

35. Interview with Debra Dawahare, October 20, 2011.

36. For analysis of the history and politics of school finance litigation at the state level, see Douglas S. Reed, *On Equal Terms: The Constitutional Politics of Educational Opportunity* (Princeton, NJ: Princeton University Press, 2001); Koski, "Of Fuzzy Standards"; Michael Paris, *Framing Equal Opportunity: Law and the Politics of School Finance Reform* (Stanford, CA: Stanford Law Books, 2010); Michael A. Rebell, *Courts and Kids: Pursuing Educational Equity through the State Courts* (Chicago: University of Chicago Press, 2009).

37. Serrano v. Priest, 487 P.2d 1241 (Cal. 1971).

38. Interview with Richard Salmon, professor emeritus, School of Education at Virginia Polytechnic Institute and State University, and expert witness and adviser to the Council for Better Education during *Rose*, November 11, 2011; Salmon's assessment of Kentucky school districts' funding, as recalled in an interview with Kern Alexander, professor, University of Illinois at Urbana-Champaign College of Education and expert witness for and adviser to the Council for Better Education during *Rose*, October 26, 2011.

39. Rebell, *Courts and Kids*, 17.

40. The Council for Better Education's original complaint against Martha Layne Collins (governor), Alice McDonald (superintendent of public instruction), Frances Jones Mills (state treasurer), Joseph W. Prather (president pro tempore of the Senate), and Donald J. Blandford (speaker of the House of Representatives), filed November 20, 1985, Franklin County Circuit Court, No. 85-CI-1759, 8; copy on file with author; hereafter, Council for Better Education Complaint.

41. Council for Better Education Complaint, 11–13.

42. Council for Better Education Complaint, 14–15.

43. Council for Better Education Complaint, 16.

44. Interview with Richard Salmon, November 11, 2011.

45. Judge Corns did offer to recuse himself given his connections to the plaintiffs, but neither side took him up on this offer because they thought his expertise would be beneficial, because it would have been difficult to find an alternative judge who did not have connections to the parties involved, and because an appeal was expected in any case; see Dove, "Acorns in a Mountain Pool," 96.

46. Judge Corns's Finding of Fact, May 31, 1988, 13.

47. Judge Corns's Supplemental Order, June 7, 1988, 2.

48. The select committee's report was later published as an article; see Kern Alexander, John Brock, Larry Forgy, James Melton, and Sylvia Watson, "Constitutional Intent: 'System,' 'Common,' and 'Efficient' as Terms of Art," *Journal of Education Finance* 15, no. 2 (1989): 142–62.

49. Judge Corns's Final Judgment, October 14, 1988, 3–5. Corns also incorporated from the select committee's report nine principles for an efficient system of common schools; see Final Judgment, 2–3.

50. Corns wrote: "The Court does not intend by this decision to provoke a confrontation with the General Assembly, the Governor, or any official of any levels of any branch of government"; see Final Judgment, 11.

51. From Bert Combs's brief, quoted in Dove, "Acorns in a Mountain Pool," 102.

52. Rose v. Council for Better Education, 790 S.W. 2d 186 (1989), at 215.

53. Ibid., at 197, 211.

54. Ibid., at 211. The Kentucky Supreme Court notably departed depart from the trial court ruling in that it did not maintain jurisdiction over the case and found that the trial judge was wrong to do so. Some saw this departure as a mistake that complicated implementation of subsequent reforms; interview with Theodore Lavit, December 2, 2011.

55. Interview with Debra Dawahare, October 20, 2011.

56. The court also included a list of the nine characteristics of an efficient system of common schools. I focus on the seven capacities that an adequate education should foster instead of these nine characteristics because the former shed light on the skills that a right to education entails.

57. Trimble and Forsaith, "Achieving Equity and Excellence," 608.

58. Interview with Richard Salmon, November 11, 2011.

59. Rose v. Council for Better Education, 790 S.W. 2d 186 (1989), at 212.

60. Scott R. Bauries emphasizes the significance of the court's finding of a positive right to education in his introduction to a series of articles commemorating *Rose's* twentieth anniversary; see Bauries, "Forward: Rights, Remedies, and *Rose*," *Kentucky Law Journal* 98 (2009–10): 708–11.

61. *Rose*, 790 S.W. 2d 186 (1989), at 212.

62. Ibid., at 190.

63. Alexander et al., "Constitutional Intent," 145.

64. *Rose*, 790 S.W. 2d 186 (1989), at 211.

65. Ibid., at 212.

66. Of course, adequacy is still preferable in this instance to equality that is achieved by leveling down, which might have brought only small improvements to some districts

while leaving others worse off, and which would have been especially problematic given that no districts had enough funding. If equality could be achieved by leveling up rather than down, it could better address positionality concerns.

67. Interviews with Kern Alexander, October 26, 2011, and Debra Dawahare, October 20, 2011.

68. See Prichard Committee for Academic Excellence, *The Path to a Larger Life: Creating Kentucky's Educational Future*, 2nd ed. (Lexington: University Press of Kentucky, 1990). For a more extended discussion of this report, see Paris, *Framing Equal Opportunity*, 176–77.

69. Bosworth, *Courts as Catalysts*, 130.

70. Interview with Cindy Heine, October 28, 2011.

71. Interview with Carolyn Witt Jones, executive director, Partnership for Successful Schools, November 29, 2011.

72. The following description of elements of KERA draws from Matthew Bosworth's summary of the curricular, governance, and financial reforms that the legislation entailed; see Bosworth, *Courts as Catalysts*, 128–34.

73. Interview with David Karem, November 18, 2011.

74. Paris, *Framing Equal Opportunity*, 205

75. Bosworth, *Courts as Catalysts*, 132–34.

76. Paris, *Framing Equal Opportunity*, 207.

77. Rose v. Council for Better Education, 790 S.W. 2d 186 (1989), at 194.

78. Paris, *Framing Equal Opportunity*, 206–7.

79. Bosworth, *Courts as Catalysts*, 134.

80. Ibid.

81. Quoted in Paris, *Framing Equal Opportunity*, 200.

82. Interview with David Karem, November 18, 2011; similar comments were expressed by other interviewees, including Jack Moreland, October 24, 2011 and Cindy Heine, October 28, 2011.

83. Interview with Mary Dean, former associate commissioner for education, Kentucky Department of Education, November 16, 2011.

84. Interview with Kevin Noland, former deputy commissioner and general counsel, Kentucky Department of Education, November 4, 2011; interview with Cindy Heine, October 28, 2011.

85. Interview with Cindy Heine, October 28, 2011.

86. Interview with Jack Moreland, October 24, 2011. The Council for Better Education sued the legislature again in 2003, but the circuit court issued a summary judgment against CBE in 2007.

87. Interview with Thomas Shelton, October 25, 2011.

88. Interview with Jack Moreland, October 24, 2011.

89. See the Annie E. Casey Foundation's Kids Count Data Center for per-pupil funding data that is cost adjusted for regional differences; available at http://datacenter.kids count.org/data/acrossstates/Rankings.aspx?loct=2&by=v&order=a&ind=5199&dtm= 11678&tf=867.

90. See Goodwin Liu, "Interstate Inequality in Educational Opportunity," *New York University Law Review* 81 (2006): 2071.

91. See Reed, *On Equal Terms*, 28–29.

92. Kentucky Department of Education Press Release, November 1, 2011, http://education.ky.gov/comm/news/Documents/R092naep.pdf.

93. Ibid.

94. Peter Schrag, *Final Test: The Battle for Adequacy in America's Schools* (New York: New Press, 2003), 66.

95. For the number of states that scored lower than, higher than, and about the same as Kentucky on NAEP reading and math in 2011, see Kentucky Department of Education Press Release, November 1, 2011.

96. Interview with Stu Silberman, executive director, Prichard Committee for Academic Excellence, October 25, 2011.

97. Interview with Kevin Noland, November 4, 2011.

98. Interview with Justin Bathon, October 13, 2011.

99. Ibid.

100. Interview with Richard Day, October 17, 2011. The founding executive director of the Prichard Committee, Robert Sexton, died in August 2010.

101. Interview with Theodore Lavit, December 2, 2011.

102. Interview with Jack Moreland, October 24, 2011.

103. Kern Alexander, "The Common School Ideal and the Limits of Legislative Authority: The Kentucky Case," *Harvard Journal on Legislation* 28, no. 2 (1991): 343.

104. For recent examples that include analysis of the *Rose* decision, see Eric A. Hanushek and Alfred A. Lindseth, *Schoolhouses, Courthouses, and Statehouses: Solving the Funding-Achievement Puzzle in America's Public Schools* (Princeton, NJ: Princeton University Press, 2009), and Martin R. West and Paul E. Peterson, eds., *School Money Trials: The Legal Pursuit of Educational Adequacy* (Washington, DC: Brookings Institution, 2007).

105. Jeremy Waldron, *Law and Disagreement* (Oxford: Oxford University Press, 1999): 232–54.

106. In Kentucky judges are chosen through nonpartisan elections.

107. Waldron offers the example here of the *Roe v. Wade* decision, which, as he describes it, gives a mere few paragraphs of attention to a woman's reproductive rights and focuses largely on procedural questions about the legitimacy of the court's involvement in the issue. See Waldron, "Core of the Case against Judicial Review," *Yale Law Journal* 115 (2006): 1382–84.

108. Waldron, "Core of the Case," 1403.

109. Ibid., 1384.

110. Jeremy Waldron, "A Rights-Based Critique of Constitutional Rights," *Oxford Journal of Legal Studies* 13 no. 1 (1993): 37.

111. Rebell, *Courts and Kids*, 6.

112. Arnold Guess, memo to selected school superintendents, April 12, 1984, on file with author; interview with Theodore Lavit, December 2, 2011.

113. Interview with Theodore Lavit, December 2, 2011.

114. Prichard Committee for Academic Excellence, *Path to a Larger Life*, xix.

115. Interview with Diana Taylor, November 8, 2011

116. John Hart Ely, *Democracy and Distrust: A Theory of Judicial Review* (Cambridge, MA: Harvard University Press, 1980).

117. Joshua Cohen, "For a Democratic Society," in *The Cambridge Companion to Rawls*, ed. Samuel Freeman (Cambridge: Cambridge University Press, 2003), 120.

118. The *Rose* decision can also be seen as a light-touch intervention despite its dramatic finding that the state's entire public education system was unconstitutional. It is light touch because the state supreme court deferred to the legislature when it came to devising a remedy, and because it did not retain jurisdiction over the reform process.

119. Corey Brettschneider, *Democratic Rights: The Substance of Self-Government* (Princeton, NJ: Princeton University Press, 2007), 137–38. Brettschneider's emphasis on the "loss to democracy" that judicial review entails, even when it is necessary to protect rights, departs from Ronald Dworkin's view, which does not recognize the added value when rights are protected through the legislative rather than the judicial process. Waldron also criticizes Dworkin on this point; see Waldron, "Core of the Case," 1398–400.

120. Relatively low levels of public engagement with education reform issues today was mentioned by a number of interviewees, including Justin Bathon, October 13, 2011; Jack Moreland, October 24, 2011; Stu Silberman, October 25, 2011; and Cindy Heine, October 28, 2011.

CHAPTER FIVE

1. For a much-debated criticism of court-based social reform that includes analysis of *Brown*, see Gerald N. Rosenberg, *The Hollow Hope: Can Courts Bring about Social Change?* (Chicago: University of Chicago Press, 1991).

2. For analysis of the history and growth of community organizing for education reform, see Dennis Shirley, "Community Organizing and Educational Change: A Reconnaissance," *Journal of Educational Change* 10, nos. 2–3 (2009): 229–37. For recent studies of organizing efforts in particular communities, see Mark R. Warren and Karen L. Mapp, *A Match on Dry Grass: Community Organizing as a Catalyst for School Reform* (New York: Oxford University Press, 2011); Kavitha Mediratta, Seema Shah, and Sara McAlister, *Community Organizing for Stronger Schools: Strategies and Successes* (Cambridge, MA: Harvard Education Press, 2009); and Jeannie Oakes and John Rogers, with Martin Lipton, *Learning Power: Organizing for Education and Justice* (New York: Teachers College Press, 2006).

3. In a recent article, Jeannie Oakes and colleagues consider how community organizing might advance students' right to education, but they do not consider how organizing groups employ rights discourse, and instead focus more broadly on the contributions to reform they stand to make; see Jeannie Oakes, John Rogers, Gary Blasi, and Martin Lipton, "Grassroots Organizing, Social Movements, and the Right to High-Quality Education," *Stanford Journal of Civil Rights and Civil Liberties* 4, no. 2 (2008): 339–71.

4. For a review of empirical research on the influence of rights claims, see Laura Beth Nielsen, "The Work of Rights and the Work Rights Do: A Critical Empirical Approach," in *The Blackwell Companion to Law and Society*, ed. Austin Sarat (Malden, MA: Blackwell, 2004), 63–79.

5. Joel Feinberg, "The Nature and Value of Rights," *The Journal of Value Inquiry* 4, no. 4 (1970): 257.

6. The following description builds on analysis from a multiyear study of youth

advocacy organizations in the San Francisco Bay area, including Coleman; see Milbrey McLaughlin, W. Richard Scott, Sarah Deschenes, Kathryn Hopkins, and Anne Newman, *Between Movement and Establishment: Organizations Advocating for Youth* (Stanford, CA: Stanford University Press, 2009); also, Sarah Deschenes, Milbrey McLaughlin, and Anne Newman, "Organizations Advocating for Youth: The Local Advantage," *New Directions for Youth Development* 117 (Spring 2008): 11–25; and Anne Newman, Sarah Deschenes, and Kathryn Hopkins, "From Agitating in the Streets to Implementing in the Suites: Understanding Education Policy Reforms Initiated by Local Advocates," *Educational Policy* 26, no. 5 (2012): 730–58.

7. According to the 2000 U.S. Census. See also Coleman's report on San Francisco's declining child population: Coleman Advocates for Children and Youth, "Families Struggle to Stay: Why Families Are Leaving San Francisco and What Can Be Done" (San Francisco: Coleman Advocates, 2006).

8. Coleman Advocates for Children and Youth, "Mission and Core Values," available at http://colemanadvocates.org/who-we-are/mission-core-values/.

9. Williams v. State of California, No. 312236 (Cal. Sup. Ct. August 14, 2000).

10. The state's lowest-performing schools (called Decile 1–3 schools), as measured by state standardized exams, must be inspected each fall by county offices of education; additional funds are available to these schools for facility repairs. For more on the terms of the *Williams* settlement, see www.decentschools.org, a website maintained by the plaintiffs' attorneys.

11. From January 2005 through September 2009, only about 80 *Williams* complaints are on record as having been filed about teacher, textbook, and facility issues in San Francisco public schools, while in Oakland over 1100 complaints were filed during this period. This tally includes quarterly complaint data from January 2005 through September 2009, with the exception of three quarters for which data were unavailable (one quarter in 2005, 2006, and 2007 each). Data are from quarterly reports collected by the author from the San Francisco Unified School District, Alameda County, and the ACLU of Southern California, which was one of the civil rights groups representing plaintiffs in the litigation. For more information on the settlement, see http://www.decentschools.org.

12. Interview with Pecolia Manigo, education justice campaign/policy director at Coleman, June 9, 2010.

13. Oakes, Rogers, Blasi, and Lipton, "Grassroots Organizing," 360–61.

14. Interview with Pecolia Manigo, June 9, 2010.

15. Interview with N'Tanya Lee, January 31, 2007.

16. Jeremy Waldron, "Rights and Needs: The Myth of Disjunction," in *Legal Rights*, ed. Austin Sarat and Thomas R. Kearns. (Ann Arbor: University of Michigan Press, 1996), 105.

17. Stuart A. Scheingold, *The Politics of Rights: Lawyers, Public Policy, and Political Change*, 2nd ed. (New Haven, CT: Yale University Press, 2007), 132.

18. Interview with Pecolia Manigo, June 9, 2010.

19. Jeremy Waldron, *Liberal Rights: Collected Papers 1981–1991* (Cambridge: Cambridge University Press, 1993), 400.

20. Coleman Advocates for Children and Youth, "Mission and Core Values," http://colemanadvocates.org/who-we-are/mission-core-values.

21. Interview with N'Tanya Lee, July 7, 2010.

22. Interview with Sandra Fewer, former Coleman staff member, December 19, 2006.

23. For more information about this campaign and the new district policy, see Coleman's Fall 2009 newsletter to families, http://colemanadvocates.org/wp-content/uploads/2010/05/Just-News-for-Families-2009-A-to-G-Victory.pdf.

24. Interview with N'Tanya Lee, January 31, 2007.

25. Interview with Sandra Fewer, December 19, 2006.

26. Ibid.

27. Interview with N'Tanya Lee, January 31, 2007.

28. Mary Ann Glendon, *Rights Talk: The Impoverishment of Political Discourse* (New York: Free Press, 1991), 137.

29. Interview with N'Tanya Lee, January 31, 2007.

30. Ibid.

31. Ibid.

32. Iris Marion Young, "Activist Challenges to Deliberative Democracy," *Political Theory* 29, no. 5 (2001): 670–90. For analysis of interest-group pluralism as a subset of the economic view of democracy, see Thomas Christiano, *The Rule of the Many: Fundamental Issues in Democratic Theory* (Boulder, CO: Westview, 1996), 140–43.

33. Young, "Activist Challenges," 673.

34. Interview with N'Tanya Lee, January 31, 2007.

35. See Coleman Advocates for Children and Youth, "A thru G Equity Plan Summary," April 20, 2009.

36. Glendon, *Rights Talk*, 9.

37. Margaret Brodkin, in a staff meeting at Coleman, August 5, 2003.

38. Archon Fung, "Deliberation before the Revolution: Toward an Ethics of Deliberative Democracy in an Unjust World," *Political Theory* 33, no. 2 (2005): 397–419.

39. Ibid., 399.

40. Ibid., 399–400.

41. Ibid., 401–4.

42. Ibid., 403.

43. For a philosophical argument about why rights claims do not serve racial minorities well in the United States and how they can be replaced with other arguments without any loss in effectiveness, see Derrick Darby, *Rights, Race, and Recognition* (Cambridge: Cambridge University Press, 2009).

44. Young, "Activist Challenges," 688.

45. Interview with N'Tanya Lee, January 31, 2007.

46. Interview with Sandra Fewer, December 19, 2006.

47. See Coleman's *Advocate Alert*, September 12, 2005, which acknowledged the vacancy and made a call for an inclusive selection process. For the announcement of this name for the campaign, see *Advocate Alert*, October 16, 2006.

48. *Advocate Alert*, February 7, 2007.

49. Project Public Education Equity meeting at Coleman, January 8, 2007.

50. Amy Gutmann and Dennis Thompson, *Democracy and Disagreement* (Cambridge, MA: Belknap, 1996).

51. Young, "Activist Challenges," 680.

52. Coleman's letter to the San Francisco Board of Education Commissioners, January 9, 2007.

53. Interview with N'Tanya Lee, July 7, 2010.

54. *Advocate Alert*, February 12, 2007.

CHAPTER SIX

1. A number of scholars in recent years have emphasized the importance of connecting reform litigation to broader community organizing and public engagement efforts, including Stuart A. Scheingold, *The Politics of Rights: Lawyers, Public Policy, and Political Change*, 2nd ed. (Ann Arbor: University of Michigan Press, 2007); Michael McCann, *Rights at Work: Pay Equity Reform and the Politics of Legal Mobilization* (Chicago: University of Chicago Press, 1994); and, with respect to education reform, Michael Paris, *Framing Equal Opportunity: Law and the Politics of School Finance Reform* (Stanford, CA: Stanford Law Books, 2010), and Michael A. Rebell, *Courts and Kids: Pursuing Educational Equity through the State Courts* (Chicago: University of Chicago Press, 2009).

2. Jeannie Oakes, John Rogers, Gary Blasi, and Martin Lipton. "Grassroots Organizing, Social Movements, and the Right to High-Quality Education," *Stanford Journal of Civil Rights and Civil Liberties* 4, no. 2 (2008): 339–71.

3. For analysis of how legal translation has shaped school finance reform efforts, see Paris, *Framing Equal Opportunity*.

4. Interview with Debra Dawahare, October 20, 2011.

5. Interview with N'Tanya Lee, July 7, 2010.

6. Interview with Jack Moreland, October 24, 2011.

7. For a collection of essays on lawyers' roles in social movements, see Austin Sarat and Stuart A. Scheingold, eds., *Cause Lawyers and Social Movements* (Stanford, CA: Stanford Law and Politics, 2006).

8. Sandra R. Levitsky, "To Lead with Law: Reassessing the Influence of Legal Advocacy Organizations in Social Movements," in *Cause Lawyers and Social Movements*, ed. Austin Sarat and Stuart A. Scheingold (Stanford, CA: Stanford Law and Politics, 2006), 146.

9. John Lewis, quoted in Thomas Hilbink, "The Profession, the Grassroots and the Elite: Cause Lawyering for Civil Rights and Freedom in the Direct Action Era," in *Cause Lawyers and Social Movements*, ed. Austin Sarat and Stuart A. Scheingold (Stanford, CA: Stanford Law and Politics, 2006).

10. Interview with Cindy Heine, October 28, 2011.

11. Interview with Debra Dawahare, October 20, 2011.

12. Interview with Tara Kini, senior staff attorney at Public Advocates, Inc., August 3, 2009.

13. For an overview of debates within this literature and an assessment of lawyers' involvement in organizing efforts, see Scott Cummings and Ingrid Eagly, "A Critical Reflection on Law and Organizing," *UCLA Law Review* 48, no. 3 (2001): 443–517.

14. For more analysis of local advocacy organizations' role in the policy implementation process after their reforms win passage, including extended discussion of Coleman's

strategies, see Anne Newman, Sarah Deschenes, and Kathryn Hopkins, "From Agitating in the Streets to Implementing in the Suites: Understanding Education Policy Reforms Initiated by Local Advocates," *Educational Policy* 26, no. 5 (2012): 730–58.

15. Interview with Pecolia Manigo, June 9, 2010.

16. Interview with Jack Moreland, October 24, 2011.

17. Public Education Network, "A Guide to Public Engagement and School Finance Litigation" (New York: Public Education Network, 2008), www.publiceducation.org/pdf/Publications/Public_Engagement/2008_Litigation_Guide.pdf.

18. For more on the Campaign for Fiscal Equity's public engagement efforts, see Michael A. Rebell, "Adequacy Litigations: A New Path to Equity?" in *Bringing Equity Back: Research for a New Era in American Educational Policy*, ed. Janice Petrovich and Amy Stuart Wells (New York: Teachers College Press, 2005), 307–15.

19. For a recent book challenging school finance litigation, see Eric A. Hanushek and Alfred A. Lindseth, *Schoolhouses, Courthouses, and Statehouses: Solving the Funding-Achievement Puzzle in America's Public Schools* (Princeton, NJ: Princeton University Press, 2009).

20. In his defense of a right to autonomy against such criticism, Richard Dagger points out how the realization of this right is necessarily a collective endeavor; see Dagger, *Civic Virtues: Rights, Citizenship, and Republican Liberalism* (Oxford: Oxford University Press, 1997), 36–40.

21. See Goodwin Liu, "Education, Equality, and National Citizenship," *Yale Law Journal* 116, no. 2 (2006): 330–411.

22. San Antonio Independent School District v. Rodriguez, 411 U.S. 1 (1973) at 49–50.

23. See Goodwin Liu, "Interstate Inequality in Educational Opportunity," *New York University Law Review* 81 (2006): 2044–128

24. See www.corestandards.org/in-the-states for current information on which states have adopted the standards.

25. See, for example, the statements of support by business, educational, and government groups posted on the Common Core Standards website, many of which focus on the need to better prepare students for the labor market in an international economy. Secretary of Education Arne Duncan's statement emphasizes this point: "There is no work more important than preparing our students to compete and succeed in a global economy." Available at: http://www.corestandards.org/about-the-standards/statements-of-support

26. For a recent article that addresses current developments toward recognition of a federal right to education and that advances a legal argument for recognizing this right, see Michael A. Rebell, "The Right to Comprehensive Educational Opportunity," *Harvard Civil Rights–Civil Liberties Law Review* 47, no. 1 (2012).

Ackerman, Bruce. *We the People: Foundations.* Cambridge, MA: Belknap, 1991.

———. *We the People: Transformations.* Cambridge, MA: Belknap, 1998.

Alexander, Kern. "The Common School Ideal and the Limits of Legislative Authority: The Kentucky Case." *Harvard Journal on Legislation* 28, no. 2 (1991): 341–66.

Alexander, Kern, John Brock, Larry Forgy, James Melton, and Sylvia Watson. "Constitutional Intent: 'System,' 'Common,' and 'Efficient' as Terms of Art." *Journal of Education Finance* 15, no. 2 (1989): 142–62.

Anderson, Elizabeth. "Rethinking Equality of Opportunity: Comment on Adam Swift's *How Not to Be a Hypocrite.*" *Theory and Research in Education* 2, no. 2 (2004): 99–110.

Aristotle. *The Politics.* Translated and edited Ernest Barker. London: Oxford University Press, 1958.

Arneson, Richard, and Ian Shapiro. "Democratic Autonomy and Religious Freedom: A Critique of *Wisconsin v. Yoder.*" In *Political Order: Nomos XXXVIII,* ed. Ian Shapiro and Russell Hardin. New York: New York University Press, 1996.

Barnett, Randy E., and Cass Sunstein. "Constitutive Commitments and Roosevelt's Second Bill of Rights: A Dialogue." *Drake Law Review* 53, no. 2 (2005): 205–29.

Bauries, Scott R. "Forward: Rights, Remedies, and Rose." *Kentucky Law Journal* 98 (2009–10): 703–16.

Berliner, David, "Our Impoverished View of Educational Research." *Teachers College Record* 108, no. 6 (2006): 949–95.

Bessette, Joseph M. *The Mild Voice of Reason: Deliberative Democracy and American National Government.* Chicago: University of Chicago Press, 1994.

Bohman, James. "Deliberative Democracy and Effective Social Freedom: Capabilities, Resources, and Opportunities." In *Deliberative Democracy: Essays on Reason and Politics,* ed. James Bohman and William Rehg. Cambridge, MA: MIT Press, 2002.

Bohman, James, and William Rehg, eds. *Deliberative Democracy: Essays on Reason and Politics.* Cambridge, MA: MIT Press, 2002.

Bosworth, Matthew H. *Courts as Catalysts: State Supreme Courts and Public School Finance Equity.* Albany, NY: SUNY Press, 2001.

Brettschneider, Corey. *Democratic Rights: The Substance of Self-Government*. Princeton, NJ: Princeton University Press, 2007.

Brighouse, Harry. *School Choice and Social Justice*. Oxford: Oxford University Press, 2000.

Brighouse, Harry, and Adam Swift. "Educational Equality versus Educational Adequacy: A Critique of Anderson and Satz." *Journal of Applied Philosophy* 26, no. 2 (2009): 117–28.

Brown, Richard D. *The Strength of a People: The Idea of an Informed Citizenry in America, 1650–1870*. Chapel Hill: University of North Carolina Press, 1996.

Callan, Eamonn. *Creating Citizens: Political Education and Liberal Democracy*. Oxford: Oxford University Press, 1997.

———. "Galston's Dilemma and *Wisconsin v. Yoder*." *Theory and Research in Education* 4, no. 3 (2006): 261–73.

Christiano, Thomas. *The Constitution of Equality: Democratic Authority and Its Limits*. Oxford: Oxford University Press, 2008.

———. *The Rule of the Many: Fundamental Issues in Democratic Theory*. Boulder, CO: Westview, 1996.

Cohen, Joshua. "Deliberation and Democratic Legitimacy." In *Deliberative Democracy: Essays on Reason and Politics*, ed. James Bohman and William Rehg. Cambridge, MA: MIT Press, 2002.

———. "For a Democratic Society." In *The Cambridge Companion to Rawls*, ed. Samuel Freeman. Cambridge: Cambridge University Press, 2003.

———. "Procedure and Substance in Deliberative Democracy." In *Deliberative Democracy: Essays on Reason and Politics*, ed. James Bohman and William Rehg. Cambridge, MA: MIT Press, 2002.

Coleman Advocates for Children and Youth. "Families Struggle to Stay: Why Families Are Leaving San Francisco and What Can Be Done." San Francisco: Coleman Advocates, 2006.

Combs, Bert T. "Creative Constitutional Law: The Kentucky School Reform Law." *Harvard Journal on Legislation* 28 (1991): 367–78.

Coons, John E., William H. Clune III, and Stephen D. Sugarman. *Private Wealth and Public Education*. Cambridge, MA: Belknap, 1970.

Cranston, Maurice. "Are There Any Human Rights?" *Daedalus* 112, no. 4 (1983): 1–17.

Cubberley, Ellwood P. *Public Education in the United States: A Study and Interpretation of American Educational History*. Cambridge, MA: Riverside, 1947.

Cummings, Scott, and Ingrid Eagly, "A Critical Reflection on Law and Organizing." *UCLA Law Review* 48, no. 3 (2001): 443–517.

Curren, Randall. *Aristotle on the Necessity of Public Education*. Lanham, MD: Rowman and Littlefield, 2000.

———. "Education as a Social Right in a Diverse Society." *Journal of Philosophy of Education* 43, no. 1 (2009): 45–56.

Dagger, Richard. *Civic Virtues: Rights, Citizenship, and Republican Liberalism*. Oxford: Oxford University Press, 1997.

Daniels, Norman. *Just Health Care*. Cambridge: Cambridge University Press, 1985.

Darby, Derrick. *Rights, Race, and Recognition*. Cambridge: Cambridge University Press, 2009.

Dee, Thomas S. "Are There Civic Returns to Education?" *Journal of Public Economics* 88 (2004): 1697–720.

Delli Carpini, Michael X., and Scott Keeter. *What Americans Know about Politics and Why It Matters*. New Haven, CT: Yale University Press, 1996.

Deschenes, Sarah, Milbrey McLaughlin, and Anne Newman, "Organizations Advocating for Youth: The Local Advantage." *New Directions for Youth Development* 117 (Spring 2008): 11–25.

Dove, Ronald G. "Acorns in a Mountain Pool: The Role of Litigation, Law, and Lawyers in Kentucky Education Reform." *Journal of Education Finance* 17, no. 1 (1991): 83–119.

Dowding, Keith, Jurgen De Wispelaere, and Stuart White, eds. *The Ethics of Stakeholding*. New York: Palgrave Macmillan, 2003.

Duncan, Arne. "The Well-Rounded Curriculum." Speech at the Arts Education Partnership National Forum, April 9, 2010. http://www2.ed.gov/news/speeches/2010/04/04092010.html.

Dworkin, Ronald. *Taking Rights Seriously*. Cambridge, MA: Harvard University Press, 1977.

Edelman, Peter B. "The Next Century of Our Constitution: Rethinking Our Duty to the Poor." *Hastings Law Journal* 39, no. 1 (1987): 1–61.

Eisgruber, Christopher L. *Constitutional Self-Government*. Cambridge, MA: Harvard University Press, 2001.

Ely, John Hart. *Democracy and Distrust: A Theory of Judicial Review*. Cambridge, MA: Harvard University Press, 1980.

Enrich, Peter. "Leaving Equality Behind: New Directions in School Finance Reform." *Vanderbilt Law Review* 48, no. 101 (1995): 101–94.

Estlund, David. *Democratic Authority: A Philosophical Framework*. Princeton, NJ: Princeton University Press, 2008.

Feinberg, Joel. "The Nature and Value of Rights." *Journal of Value Inquiry* 4, no. 4 (1970): 243–60.

Felstiner, William L. F., Richard L. Abel, and Austin Sarat. "The Emergence and Transformation of Disputes: Naming, Blaming, Claiming." *Law and Society Review* 15, nos. 3/4 (1980–81): 631–54.

Forbath, William E.. "Constitutional Change and the Politics of History." *Yale Law Journal* 108, no. 8 (1999): 1917–30.

———. "Why Is This Rights Talk Different from All Other Rights Talk? Demoting the Court and Reimagining the Constitution." Review of *The Partial Constitution*, by Cass Sunstein. *Stanford Law Review* 46, no. 6 (1994): 1771–805.

Fung, Archon. "Deliberation before the Revolution: Toward an Ethics of Deliberative Democracy in an Unjust World." *Political Theory* 33, no. 2 (2005): 397–419.

———. *Empowered Participation: Reinventing Urban Democracy*. Princeton, NJ: Princeton University Press, 2004.

Galston, William A. "Civic Education in the Liberal State." In *Philosophers on Educa-*

tion: New Historical Perspectives, ed. Amelie Oksenberg Rorty. London: Routledge, 1998.

———. *Liberal Purpose: Goods, Virtues, and Diversity in the Liberal State*. Cambridge: Cambridge University Press, 1991.

———. "Political Knowledge, Political Engagement, and Civic Education." *Annual Review of Political Science* 4 (2001): 217–34.

Glendon, Mary Ann. *Rights Talk: The Impoverishment of Political Discourse*. New York: Free Press, 1991.

Goodin, Robert. *Reflective Democracy*. Oxford: Oxford University Press, 2003.

Gutmann, Amy. "Civic Education and Social Diversity." *Ethics* 105, no. 3 (1995): 557–79.

———. "Deliberative Democracy and Majority Rule: Reply to Waldron." In *Deliberative Democracy and Human Rights*, ed. Harold Hongju Koh and Ronald C. Slye. New Haven, CT: Yale University Press, 1999.

———. *Democratic Education*. Princeton, NJ: Princeton University Press, 1999.

Gutmann, Amy, and Dennis Thompson. *Democracy and Disagreement*. Cambridge, MA: Belknap, 1996.

Habermas, Jürgen. *Between Facts and Norms: Contributions to a Discourse Theory of Law and Democracy*. Translated by William Rehg. Cambridge, MA: MIT Press, 1996.

Hanushek, Eric A., and Alfred A. Lindseth. *Schoolhouses, Courthouses, and Statehouses: Solving the Funding-Achievement Puzzle in America's Public Schools*. Princeton, NJ: Princeton University Press, 2009.

Hayward, Clarissa Rile. "Doxa and Deliberation." *Critical Review of International Social and Political Philosophy* 7, no. 1 (2004): 1–24.

Heise, Michael. "State Constitutions, School Finance Litigation, and the 'Third Wave': From Equity to Adequacy." *Temple Law Review* 68 (1995): 1151–76.

———. "The Story of *San Antonio Independent School Dist. v. Rodriguez*: School Finance, Local Control, and Constitutional Limits." Cornell Law Faculty Publications, Paper 76 (2007). http://scholarship.law.cornell.edu/lsrp_papers/76.

Hilbink, Thomas. "The Profession, the Grassroots and the Elite: Cause Lawyering for Civil Rights and Freedom in the Direct Action Era." In *Cause Lawyers and Social Movements*, ed. Austin Sarat and Stuart A. Scheingold. Stanford, CA: Stanford Law and Politics, 2006.

Hochschild, Jennifer, and Nathan Scovronick. *The American Dream and the Public Schools*. Oxford: Oxford University Press, 2003.

Holmes, Stephen, and Cass Sunstein. *The Cost of Rights: Why Liberty Depends on Taxes*. New York: W. W. Norton, 1999.

Hunter, Molly A. "All Eyes Forward: Public Engagement and Educational Reform in Kentucky." *Journal of Law and Education* 28, no. 4 (1999): 485–516.

Jacobs, Lesley A. *Rights and Deprivation*. Oxford: Oxford University Press, 1993.

Jefferson, Thomas. "A Bill for the More General Diffusion of Knowledge." In *The Educational Works of Thomas Jefferson*, ed. Roy J. Honeywell. Cambridge, MA: Harvard University Press, 1931.

Jencks, Christopher. "Whom Must We Treat Equally for Educational Opportunity to Be Equal?" *Ethics* 98, no. 3 (1988): 518–33.

Kaestle, Carl F. "Equal Educational Opportunity and the Federal Government: A Response to Goodwin Liu." *Yale Law Journal Pocket Part* 116, no. 152 (2006).
———. *Pillars of the Republic: Common Schools and American Society, 1780–1860.* New York: Hill and Wang, 1983.
Katz, Michael S. "Is There a Right to Education? A Philosophical Analysis through U.S. Lenses." In *Education, Democracy, and the Moral Life,* ed. Michael S. Katz, Susan Verducci, and Gert Biesta. New York: Springer, 2008.
Kennedy, David M. *Freedom from Fear: The American People in Depression and War, 1929–1945.* New York: Oxford University Press, 1999.
Koski, William S. "Of Fuzzy Standards and Institutional Constraints: A Re-Examination of the Jurisprudential History of Educational Finance Reform Litigation." *Santa Clara Law Review* 43, no. 4 (2003): 1185–298
Koski, William S., and Rob Reich, "When 'Adequate' Isn't: The Retreat from Equity in Educational Law and Policy and Why It Matters." *Emory Law Journal* 56, no. 3 (2006): 545–617.
Kramer, Larry. *The People Themselves: Popular Constitutionalism and Judicial Review.* New York: Oxford University Press, 2004.
Labaree, David. "Public Goods, Private Goods: The American Struggle over Educational Goals." *American Educational Research Journal* 34, no. 1 (1997): 39–81.
Levinson, Meira. *The Demands of Liberal Education.* Oxford: Oxford University Press, 1999.
Levitsky, Sandra R. "To Lead with Law: Reassessing the Influence of Legal Advocacy Organizations in Social Movements." In *Cause Lawyers and Social Movements,* ed. Austin Sarat and Stuart A. Scheingold. Stanford, CA: Stanford Law and Politics, 2006.
Liu, Goodwin. "Education, Equality, and National Citizenship." *Yale Law Journal* 116, no. 2 (2006): 330–411.
———. "Interstate Inequality in Educational Opportunity." *New York University Law Review* 81 (2006): 2044–128.
———. "National Citizenship and the Promise of Equal Educational Opportunity." *Yale Law Journal Pocket Part* 116, no. 145 (2006). www.yalelawjournal.org/images/pdfs/77.pdf.
MacMullen, Ian. *Faith in Schools?* Princeton, NJ: Princeton University Press, 2007.
Marshall, T. H. "Citizenship and Social Class." In *Class, Citizenship, and Social Development: Essays by T. H. Marshall.* Garden City, NY: Doubleday, 1964.
McCann, Michael. *Rights at Work: Pay Equity Reform and the Politics of Legal Mobilization.* Chicago: University of Chicago Press, 1994.
McDonnell, Lorraine M., and M. Stephen Weatherford. *Practical Deliberation in Local School Districts: A South Carolina Experiment.* Los Angeles: Center for the Study of Evaluation, University of California–Los Angeles, 2000. http://www.cse.ucla.edu/products/Reports/TECH520.pdf
———. "Seeking a New Politics of Education." In *Rediscovering the Democratic Purposes of Education,* ed. Lorraine M. McDonnell, P. Michael Timpane, and Roger Benjamin. Lawrence: University Press of Kansas, 2000.
McLaughlin, Milbrey, W. Richard Scott, Sarah Deschenes, Kathryn Hopkins, and Anne

Newman. *Between Movement and Establishment: Organizations Advocating for Youth.* Stanford, CA: Stanford University Press, 2009.

Mediratta, Kavitha, Seema Shah, and Sara McAlister. *Community Organizing for Stronger Schools: Strategies and Successes.* Cambridge, MA: Harvard Education Press, 2009.

Michelman, Frank I. "Foreword: On Protecting the Poor through the Fourteenth Amendment." *Harvard Law Review* 83, no. 7 (1969): 7–59.

Newman, Anne. "A Democratic Framework for Educational Rights." *Educational Theory* 62, no. 1 (2012): 7–23.

——. "All Together Now? Some Egalitarian Concerns about Deliberation and Education Policy-Making." *Theory and Research in Education* 7, no. 1 (2009): 65–87.

——. "Transforming a Moral Right into a Legal Right: The Case of School Finance Litigation and the Right to Education." *Philosophy of Education Yearbook 2006,* ed. Daniel Vokey, 82–90. Urbana, IL: Philosophy of Education Society.

Newman, Anne, Sarah Deschenes, and Kathryn Hopkins. "From Agitating in the Streets to Implementing in the Suites: Understanding Education Policy Reforms Initiated by Local Advocates." *Educational Policy* 26, no. 5 (2012): 730–58.

Nie, Norman, and D. Sunshine Hillygus. "Education and Democratic Citizenship." In *Making Good Citizens: Education and Civil Society,* ed. Diane Ravitch and Joseph P. Viteritti. New Haven, CT: Yale University Press, 2001.

Nie, Norman H., Jane Junn, and Kenneth Stehlik-Barry. *Education and Democratic Citizenship in America.* Chicago: University of Chicago Press, 1996.

Nielsen, Laura Beth. "The Work of Rights and the Work Rights Do: A Critical Empirical Approach." In *The Blackwell Companion to Law and Society,* ed. Austin Sarat. Malden, MA: Blackwell, 2004.

Nozick, Robert. *Anarchy, State, and Utopia.* New York: Basic Books, 1974.

Oakes, Jeannie, and John Rogers, with Martin Lipton. *Learning Power: Organizing for Education and Justice.* New York: Teachers College Press, 2006.

Oakes, Jeannie, John Rogers, and Gary Blasi, and Martin Lipton. "Grassroots Organizing, Social Movements, and the Right to High-Quality Education." *Stanford Journal of Civil Rights and Civil Liberties* 4, no. 2 (2008): 339–71.

Orfield, Gary, John Kucsera, and Genevieve Siegel-Hawley. *E Pluribus . . . Separation: Deepening Double Segregation for More Students.* Los Angeles: The Civil Rights Project/Proyecto Derechos Civiles, 2012.

Pangle, Lorraine Smith, and Thomas L. Pangle. *The Learning of Liberty: The Educational Ideas of the American Founders.* Lawrence: University Press of Kansas, 1993.

Paris, Michael. *Framing Equal Opportunity: Law and the Politics of School Finance Reform.* Stanford, CA: Stanford Law Books, 2010.

Pateman, Carole. "Freedom and Democratization: Why Basic Income Is to Be Preferred to Basic Capital." In *The Ethics of Stakeholding,* ed. Keith Dowding, Jurgen De Wispelaere, and Stuart White. New York: Palgrave Macmillan, 2003.

Pocock, J. A. *The Machiavellian Moment.* Princeton, NJ: Princeton University Press, 1975.

Popkin, Samuel L., and Michael A. Dimock. "Political Knowledge and Citizen Competence." In *Citizen Competence and Democratic Institutions,* ed. Stephen L. Elkin and Karol Edward Soltan. University Park: Pennsylvania State University Press, 1999.

Prichard Committee for Academic Excellence. *The Path to a Larger Life: Creating Kentucky's Educational Future*. 2nd ed. Lexington: University Press of Kentucky, 1990.

Public Education Network. "A Guide to Public Engagement and School Finance Litigation." New York: Public Education Network, 2008. www.publiceducation.org/pdf/Publications/Public_Engagement/2008_Litigation_Guide.pdf.

Rawls, John. *Political Liberalism*. New York: Columbia University Press, 1996.

———. *A Theory of Justice*. Rev. ed. Cambridge, MA: Harvard University Press, 1999.

Rebell, Michael A. "Adequacy Litigations: A New Path to Equity?" In *Bringing Equity Back: Research for a New Era in American Educational Policy*, ed. Janice Petrovich and Amy Stuart Wells. New York: Teachers College Press, 2005.

———. *Courts and Kids: Pursuing Educational Equity through the State Courts*. Chicago: University of Chicago Press, 2009.

———. "The Right to Comprehensive Educational Opportunity." *Harvard Civil Rights–Civil Liberties Law Review* 47, no. 1 (2012): 47–117.

Reed, Douglas S. *On Equal Terms: The Constitutional Politics of Educational Opportunity*. Princeton, NJ: Princeton University Press, 2001.

Reich, Rob. *Bridging Liberalism and Multiculturalism in American Education*. Chicago: University of Chicago Press, 2002.

Roosevelt, Franklin D. "Message to the Congress on the State of the Union," January 11, 1944. In *The Public Papers and Addresses of Franklin D. Roosevelt*, vol. 13, ed. Samuel I. Rosenman. New York: Harper and Brothers, 1950.

Rosenberg, Gerald N. *The Hollow Hope: Can Courts Bring About Social Change?* Chicago: University of Chicago Press, 1991.

Rosenberg, Shawn W. "Types of Discourse and the Democracy of Deliberation." In *Deliberation, Participation and Democracy: Can the People Govern?* ed. Shawn W. Rosenberg. New York: Palgrave Macmillan, 2007.

Rush, Benjamin. "Thoughts upon the Mode of Education Proper in a Republic." In *Essays on Education in the Early Republic*, ed. Frederick Rudolph. Cambridge, MA: Belknap, 1965.

Ryan, Susan, Anthony S. Bryk, Gudelia Lopez, Kimberly P. Williams, Kathleen Hall, and Stuart Luppescu. *Charting Reform: LSCs — Local Leadership at Work*. Chicago: Consortium on Chicago School Research, 1997.

Sanders, Lynn M. "Against Deliberation." *Political Theory* 25, no. 3 (1997): 347–76.

Sarat, Austin, and Stuart A. Scheingold, eds. *Cause Lawyers and Social Movements*. Stanford, CA: Stanford Law and Politics, 2006.

Satz, Debra. "Equality, Adequacy and Education for Citizenship." *Ethics* 117, no. 4 (2007): 623–48.

Scheingold, Stuart A. *The Politics of Rights: Lawyers, Public Policy, and Political Change*, 2nd ed. Ann Arbor, MI: University of Michigan Press, 2007.

Schrag, Peter. *Final Test: The Battle for Adequacy in America's Schools*. New York: New Press, 2003.

Schumpeter, Joseph. *Capitalism, Socialism, and Democracy*. New York: Harper and Brothers, 1947.

Sen, Amartya. "Elements of a Theory of Human Rights." *Philosophy and Public Affairs* 32, no. 4 (2004): 315–56.

———. "Equality of What?" The Tanner Lecture on Human Values, Stanford University, May 22, 1979. http://www.tannerlectures.utah.edu/lectures/sen80.pdf.

Sexton, Robert F. *Mobilizing Citizens for Better Schools*. New York: Teachers College Press, 2004.

Shapiro, Ian. "Enough of Deliberation: Politics Is about Interests and Power." In *Deliberative Politics: Essays on Democracy and Disagreement*, ed. Stephen Macedo. New York: Oxford University Press, 1999.

———. *The State of Democratic Theory*. Princeton, NJ: Princeton University Press, 2003.

Shirley, Dennis. "Community Organizing and Educational Change: A Reconnaissance." *Journal of Educational Change* 10, nos. 2–3 (2009): 229–37.

———. *Community Organizing for Urban School Reform*. Austin: University of Texas Press, 1997.

Shue, Henry. *Basic Rights: Subsistence, Affluence, and U.S. Foreign Policy*. Princeton, NJ: Princeton University Press, 1980.

Southern Education Foundation. *No Time to Lose: Why America Needs an Education Amendment to the US Constitution to Improve Public Education*. Atlanta: Southern Education Foundation, 2009.

Sunstein, Cass. *The Partial Constitution*. Cambridge, MA: Harvard University Press, 1993.

———. *The Second Bill of Rights: FDR's Unfinished Revolution and Why We Need It More than Ever*. New York: Basic Books, 2004.

Trimble, C. Scott, and Andrew C. Forsaith, "Achieving Equity and Excellence in KY Education." *University of Michigan Journal of Law Reform* 28 no. 3 (1994–95): 599–653.

Tyack, David B., ed. *Turning Points in American Educational History*. Waltham, MA: Blaisdell, 1967.

Tyack, David, Thomas James, and Aaron Benavot. *Law and the Shaping of Public Education, 1785–1954*. Madison: University of Wisconsin Press, 1987.

United Nations General Assembly. *Universal Declaration of Human Rights*. December 10, 1948. http://www.un.org/Overview/rights.html.

Van Parijs, Philippe. *Real Freedom for All*. Oxford: Clarendon, 1995.

———. "Why Surfers Should Be Fed: The Liberal Case for an Unconditional Basic Income." *Philosophy and Public Affairs* 20, no. 2 (1991): 101–31.

Verba, Sidney, Kay Lehman Schlozman, and Henry E. Brady. *Voice and Equality: Civic Voluntarism in American Politics*. Cambridge, MA: Harvard University Press, 1995.

Waldron, Jeremy. "The Core of the Case against Judicial Review." *Yale Law Journal* 115 (2006): 1346–1406.

———. *Law and Disagreement*. Oxford: Oxford University Press, 1999.

———. *Liberal Rights: Collected Papers, 1981–1991*. Cambridge: Cambridge University Press, 1993.

———. "Rights." In *A Companion to Contemporary Political Philosophy*, ed. Robert E. Goodin and Philip Pettit. Oxford: Blackwell, 1993.

———. "Rights and Needs: The Myth of Disjunction." In *Legal Rights*, ed. Austin Sarat and Thomas R. Kearns. Ann Arbor: University of Michigan Press, 1996.

———. "A Rights-Based Critique of Constitutional Rights." *Oxford Journal of Legal Studies* 13 no. 1 (1993): 18–51.

Warren, Mark. *Dry Bones Rattling: Community Building to Revitalize American Democracy.* Princeton, NJ: Princeton University Press, 2001.

Warren, Mark R., and Karen L. Mapp. *A Match on Dry Grass: Community Organizing as a Catalyst for School Reform.* New York: Oxford University Press, 2011.

Weatherford, M. Stephen, and Lorraine McDonnell. "Deliberation with a Purpose: Reconnecting Communities and Schools." In *Deliberation, Participation and Democracy: Can the People Govern?* ed. Shawn W. Rosenberg. New York: Palgrave Macmillan, 2007.

West, Martin R., and Paul E. Peterson, eds. *School Money Trials: The Legal Pursuit of Educational Adequacy.* Washington, DC: Brookings Institution, 2007.

Wood, Gordon S. *The Creation of the American Republic, 1776–1787.* Chapel Hill: University of North Carolina Press, 1998.

Young, Iris Marion. "Activist Challenges to Deliberative Democracy." *Political Theory* 29, no. 5 (2001): 670–90.

———. *Inclusion and Democracy.* New York: Oxford University Press, 2000.

Yudof, Mark G., David K. Kirp, Betsy Levin, and Rachel F. Moran. *Educational Policy and the Law.* 4th ed. Belmont, CA: Thomson Learning, 2002.

INDEX

Ackerman, Bruce, 2, 126n6
acquiescence of the oppressed, 68
activism: versus deliberative democracy, 97–100, 104; deliberative versus nondeliberative, 90; deradicalization of social movements and, 110
adequacy of education: content of education and, 59; determination of, 15–16; versus equality, 48, 53, 55–60, 65, 71, 76, 81, 133–34n66; in Kentucky post-*Rose*, 80–81; purpose of, 81; *Rose* case and, 65, 74; standards of comparison and, 81; student capacities and, 74, 133n56
advocacy. *See* activism; litigation, education-related
Alexander, Kern, 66, 72, 75, 84
Algebra Project, 108
American Revolution, public education and, 44–47
Anderson, Elizabeth, 58, 59
Aristotle, 31
Arneson, Richard, 34
Ashland Oil, Kentucky education reform and, 77
autonomy: civic education and, 32–33; civic equality and, 35; civic participation and, 124n44, 124n51; cognitive, 35–39, 42, 75; critical reasoning and, 38–39; meaning of, 124n51; obstacles to, 35–36; public and private spheres and, 35, 123n35; *Rose* case and, 75; skills that constitute, 37; voting and, 35–39

Bathon, Justin, 131n9
Beckner, William M., 63

Blair, Henry William, 49
Blair Bill (1880s), 49
Blandford, Donald, 73
Bohman, James, 17, 119n14
Brettschneider, Corey, 28, 86–87, 136n119
Brighouse, Harry, 20, 31, 123n30
Brodkin, Margaret, 90
Brown v. Board of Education, 75, 88

Callan, Eamonn, 32, 33, 39, 123n37
Campaign for Fiscal Equity (New York), 113
Chicago, LSCs in, 20–21
Children's Amendment (San Francisco), 91, 102
Children's Defense Fund, 96
Christiano, Thomas, 118n5
citizenship: cognitive demands of, 38–39, 42, 43–44; duty of participation and, 31–32, 44; education for equal, 33–35, 48, 75, 115–16; thin view of, 32; virtuous, 44–45; welfare rights and, 28. *See also* deliberative democracy
civic education: cognitive autonomy and, 35; content of, 5; critical reasoning and, 39; duties of citizenship and, 31–32; literature on, 4–5; parental authority and, 42; popular government and, 45–46; public reason and, 40; *Rose* case and, 75; skills fostered by, 25; state interests and, 34; state's obligation and, 35, 42; thin view of citizenship and, 32–33; third-sector organizations and, 114–15; types of democracy and, 25
civic participation: autonomy and, 124n44, 124n51; educational attainment and,

151